Japanese business leaders

Japanese business leaders

Andrew Kakabadse

Professor, International Management Development Centre
Director, International Management Development Centre
Cranfield School of Management

Lola Okazaki-Ward

Senior Research Officer
International Management Development Centre
Cranfield School of Management

Andrew Myers

Senior Research Officer
International Management Development Centre
Cranfield School of Management

INTERNATIONAL THOMSON BUSINESS PRESS
I(T)P An International Thomson Publishing Company

London • Bonn • Boston • Johannesburg • Madrid • Melbourne • Mexico City • New York • Paris
Singapore • Tokyo • Toronto • Albany, NY • Belmont, CA • Cincinnati, OH • Detroit, MI

Japanese business leaders
Copyright © 1996 Andrew Kakabadse, Lola Okazaki-Ward,
Andrew Myers

First published 1996 by International Thomson Business Press

I(T)P   A division of International Thomson Publishing Inc.
        The ITP logo is a trademark under licence

British Library Cataloguing-in-Publication Data
A catalogue record for this book is available from the British Library

First edition 1996

Typeset by J&L Composition Ltd, Filey, North Yorkshire
Printed in the UK

ISBN 1–86152–024–7

International Thomson Business Press   International Thomson Business Press
Berkshire House   20 Park Plaza
168–173 High Holborn   13th Floor
London WC1V 7AA   Boston MA 02116
UK   USA

http://www.thomson.com/itbp.html

Contents

Tables and figure

TABLES

FIGURE

Acknowledgements

The research team at Cranfield acknowledges the help, support and co-operation given by our partner at the Japan Management Association who carried out the main part of the questionnaire survey on our behalf in Japan, and produced the report on its part of the questionnaire survey in Japanese in co-operation with the team. Particular thanks go to Masamichi Shimizu of the Japan Management Association for his extraordinary effort in bringing this survey to successful fruition. The team would also like to thank Keizai Doyukai of Japan who have not only been instrumental in providing the team access to its members for interviewing but are also providing opportunities for holding a discussion and presentation of our comparative Europe–Japan research results in Japan. Thanks also to British Airways and ICI Japan whose sponsorship made it possible for us to come to Japan to undertake this interesting survey. A very special thank you to Doctor Jinnosuke Miyai, President of the Japan Productivity Centre for Socio-Economic Development, Doctor Jutaka Kume, Chairman of Nissan Motor Co. Ltd, and Professor Shuhei Aida, Visiting Professor at Cranfield University, whose support and assistance have been absolutely invaluable. Finally, but not least, the team are grateful to the managers who completed the research questionnaire and especially those who kindly gave their time to be interviewed for the research.

In writing the book we acknowledge the generous help given by Sumitomo Corporation UK which enabled the authors to keep abreast with developments in Japan.

Introduction

> Management, from now on, needs both to adhere to a long-term perspective, which is a strength of Japanese companies, and respect stockholders' rights. Establishment of corporate selfhood requires that the function of exchanging information with stakeholders be enhanced, and a consensus regarding a standard of conduct and distribution of the fruits of commercial success be achieved.
>
> (Keizai Dôyûkai, *Establishment of Corporate Selfhood and Creative Management*)

Professor Suzuki, writing in the November 1989 issue of the *Journal of Management Development*, questioned whether Japanese CEOs can be trained (Suzuki 1989). Due to the 'lifetime' employment experience in mid- to large-sized Japanese corporates, the current generation of Japanese CEOs have emerged through the internal promotion ladder, requiring them to have spent years of tacit but nevertheless fierce competition with their peers. Enhanced by the seniority-driven practice of career pathing, the top managers have been grown in the same company, sharing the experience of the challenges of junior, middle and senior management. Suzuki's point is that the intensity and discipline applied to networking in Japan is untrainable, as the meaningful nature of development is on-the-job.

However, a more recent and completely contrasting view is offered by Kiichi Mochizuki (1994), Chairman of the Pacific Institute, at a Royal Society of Arts lecture stating that 'a major flaw of life-time employment, if practised, is that the corporation becomes a social unit, a closed village which rejects the inclusion of any outsider, including the shareholder' (p. 39). He continues with the view that the continuous linear growth which epitomized Japanese industry for forty years (1950–1990), characterized by the unity and loyalty of employees to the corporation, is a phenomenon equally experienced in the West, quoting IBM as an example, the point being however, that Japan has experienced a longer phase of growth. In Mochizuki's opinion, this state of affairs cannot continue. The thinking for the future will need to be more open and strategic.

Corporate boards in Japan will not be able to afford to be filled with insiders and bank representatives. Shareholders will simply not tolerate such a state of affairs. Further, long-term investment at the expense of short-term profits is manageable under conditions of continuous growth, but cannot be sustained in conditions of diminishing revenues and rising costs. As a result, Mochizuki postulates that the consensus-driven organization is likely to be superseded by the stakeholder-driven organization, comprising stakeholders, ranging from shareholders, trade unions, environmental interest groups, customers and other numerous special interest groups, all potentially making irreconcilable demands on an ever beleaguered Japanese leadership. The emerging world view of corporations is one of a philosophy needing to promote stakeholder value.

The two viewpoints of the challenges facing Japanese business leaders, namely being accomplished at networking, and, in contrast, having to face up to making difficult people-oriented decisions which are likely to disrupt accepted ways of working, provide for an interesting perspective as to the future developmental requirements of Japanese managers. With such contrast in mind, a study of Japanese business leaders has been undertaken by the International Management Development Centre, at Cranfield School of Management, the results of which are outlined in this study report.

This work is divided into three parts. Part I provides a brief overview of recent Japanese business, political and social history, emphasizing the circumstances that have led to the current questioning of present employment practices in Japan. Within such a context, the leadership challenge facing Japanese business organizations is highlighted. In Part II, attention is given to examining how senior Japanese managers are responding to the leadership challenges they face. Issues concerning visioning, quality of dialogue and trust are discussed. Further, comparative results are presented exploring Japanese leader behaviour across the three sectors of manufacturing, retail and services, and equally how particular styles of Japanese business leaders impact on European managers. As a consequence of the results of this study, consideration is given in Part III as to the implications for management development of senior and high potential Japanese managers.

Part I

Japan: history, politics, economy and society

Chapter 1

Brief history of development to 1945

Paradoxically, Japan's relations with Western countries have continued to be profoundly influenced by a sense of isolation. The circumstances of the move – from seclusion and complete vulnerability to the position of one of the world's most powerful nations, both pre-war and post-war – failed to dispel a feeling that, in the end, Japan stood alone.

(J. E. Hunter, *The Emergence of Modern Japan*)

KEY ISSUES

In 1867 a revolution called the Meiji Restoration brought to an end the centuries-old feudal system ruled by military dictatorship in Japan, and ushered in the modern period. This chapter briefly describes the antecedent conditions which prevailed in pre-Restoration Japan in order to set the scene for the subsequent period of modernization, and how this transformation was managed by a hard-nosed pragmatism of the Japanese in order to avoid the possibility of colonization by the Western powers. This siege mentality, the legacy of the unequal treaties Japan was forced to conclude with the Western powers in the 1850s, was to motivate generations of Japanese to strive to 'catch up and overtake' the West throughout the modern period. Industrialization, pump-primed by the government initially, took off in the 1890s, and, stimulated by the two wars in which Japan engaged successfully at the turn of the century, progressed rapidly in the first two decades of the twentieth century, which also saw the emergence of the family-owned conglomerates called *zaibatsu* that dominated the Japanese economy in the period up to the beginning of World War II.

THE PRE-MODERN PERIOD

Japan, comprising four major islands and many small ones, has a land mass of about one and a half times that of the UK, but the mountainous terrain leaves only approximately one-sixth of the total area suitable for the human activities that support its population. In effect, a country poor in raw materials and agricultural potential supports a population of 124 million in a habitable land mass not much bigger than the Republic of Ireland. Geographic location has had a considerable impact on the historic development of Japan. Japan's early history is one of being substantively influenced by the Chinese mainland through the conduit of Korea. Two major philosophical influences on Japan, Confucianism and Buddhism, were brought to Japan around the fifth century with the Chinese ideographs, and patriarchal social and legal systems of the advanced Chinese being adopted by the eighth century. Japan was eclectic in its adoption of the alien culture and integrated it with its own to produce a new and richer cultural synthesis.

A more recent feature of Japan's history is a self-imposed isolation from the rest of the world, which lasted for over two hundred years until almost the end of the pre-modern period known as the Edo Period (1603–1867). During this era of feudal government run by a military dictatorship, Japan developed a unique cultural identity in its traditions and social institutions. As its isolation coincided with the period of industrialization in the West, Japan remained largely an agrarian society, supported by well-developed commercial activities, and high levels of artistic skills in craft work. Limited trade under strict official control was allowed with the Chinese and Dutch through the single trading port of Nagasaki. During this period of isolation (1639–1953), the Tokugawa Shogunate government de facto ruled the country from Edo, today's Tokyo, while the imperial court was maintained, although on a shoestring budget in Kyoto, to enhance the Shogunate authority. The country was divided into some 280 domains of differing sizes, each administered independently by a territorial baron (*daimyô*) who nevertheless owed his allegiance to the Shogun in Edo. In return for that allegiance he was given the right to exact tax, in the form of rice, from the farmers in his domain. The system of 'alternative attendance', by which the barons had to alternate their residence between their domains and Edo where their wives and children were kept permanently as the hostages of the Shogunate, ensured their compliance. The system also supported a basic form of communication between the political centre and the provinces.

The population was divided into the four major caste-like hierarchical status groups of warriors, farmers, craftsmen and traders. The major status distinction was drawn between the warrior class, about 7 per cent of the population, and the remainder, who were commoners, and across which social mobility was limited. The warriors, craftsmen and merchants dwelt in commercial and castle towns. Edo, the Shogunal capital, was the archetypical castle town which became a huge administrative centre of about one million people by the early eighteenth century. Osaka, in contrast, developed as the centre of commodity distribution, particularly rice, and grew to a population of about 500,000. It was nicknamed 'the kitchen of Japan', with its own brand of commercial culture. About 10 per cent of Japan's population lived in cities of over 10,000 inhabitants (Hall 1968).

With large urban centres developing, the commercial activities by the merchant class expanded to meet the need of the consumers, and large merchant houses such as Mitsui and Sumitomo emerged as early as the beginning of the eighteenth century. The warrior class, whose income, in the form of an annual stipend of rice, was fixed for all times, became progressively more impoverished and deeply indebted to the merchant class which prospered.

The highly stratified society was nevertheless tightly controlled by the warrior class through their adoption of Confucianism as the orthodox philosophy. Confucianism demanded unquestioning devotion and loyalty from subordinates to their superiors, and conformity to group values that especially prevailed in the villages due to the imposition of the rice tax on farming communities by the *daimyô*. However, despite the revenue support and without any battle to fight, the warrior class was reduced to an impoverished but proud body of administrators. Towards the end of the Edo period, there developed the major contradiction in the rigid socio-political system in which the ruling class had power but were deeply in debt to the rich but powerless merchant class. This eventually helped to undermine the rigidity of the social order.

The beginning of the end of the feudal system was signalled when America demanded the opening of Japan through gunboat diplomacy in 1853. The Tokugawa Shogunate, aware of its inadequacy to withstand a possible military engagement, bowed to the pressure, opening the floodgate for other Western powers. Towards the end of the 1850s the Shogunate government was also forced to sign a treaty with Russia, Great Britain and France. Fundamentally, the Treaty deprived Japan of the right to impose tax on imports and to have jurisdiction over foreign nationals on its own soil. It did so without recourse to imperial authority which brought the anti-Shogunate elements of the country together, toppling the Shogunate by the Meiji Restoration in 1867. This ushered in the modern period with the monarchy restored to the position of political authority.

MODERNIZATION OF JAPAN

The subsequent modernization, modelled on Western social, political, judicial and economic institutions and industrial technology, was based on the hard-nosed pragmatism of Japan's new leaders. They understood that the adoption of the institutional trappings of Western civilization was the only way open to the repeal of the so-called 'unequal treaties' signed by the Tokugawa Shogunate with the Western powers. They also appreciated that an effective way to prevent colonization by the West was to build Japan up as an industrially and militarily strong, modern nation (Hunter 1989), setting out to transform Japan under the slogan of *Fukoku Kyôhei* ('rich country, strong armed forces'). The feudal class system was abolished to facilitate social, occupational and geographical mobility. National systems of conscription, education and fiscal taxation were introduced as the basic three policies to build a modern nation state. The cabinet system was adopted by the government in 1885, and the constitution, modelled on Prussia's, was promulgated in 1889, followed in the next year by the opening of the first parliamentary session in a new diet. The election was based on a limited male franchise, with parliament having no power over the military or over foreign affairs. Further, the cabinet was not accountable to the diet (Toyota 1964). In the same year, the Rescript on Education was issued re-imposing distinctive Confucian and feudalistic values on the conduct of the population. These values were further strengthened in the Common Codes based on the patriarchal family model, which came into effect in the late 1890s. Japan was eclectic in its adoption of Western systems in building a modern state, but the feudal values reasserted themselves to become the guiding philosophical principles.

Japan's early desire and effort to 'catch up and overtake' the West has remained a strong motivating factor for Japan's modernization and development throughout this century. Though not widely recognized, the deep humiliation inflicted upon Japan by the Western nations by the 'unequal' treaties, has left a profound scar on the national psyche (Terasawa 1995), captured by the slogan *Wakon Yôsai* ('the Japanese spirit and Western technology') which appeared in the early 1880s to counter the earlier adoption of the Western social and political values. Industrialization became the 'national objective' (Minami 1994) and the ruling warrior class of the previous age which had disdained commercial activities as demeaning to their status, nevertheless took to industrial and commercial activities for the sake of the 'national good' (Hunter 1989).

Accompanying these developments, the culture of obedience to authority continued to be fostered as much through education as through other social levers. Education was one of the major means which accommodated continuity and change. The system of national elementary schooling was laid down as early as 1872, through being grafted onto thousands of small private schools called *terakoya* (temple schools) which had emerged to provide basic literary and numeracy to the children of the commoner classes during the Tokugawa period. A relatively high literacy rate, estimated to be around 27 per cent at the end of the period (Dore 1965) was an important contributing factor in Japan's success in modernization. The first national university, in Tokyo, was established in 1877 out of the Shogunal higher schools. It was upgraded to an Imperial University in 1887 and comprised five faculties, one of which was engineering, the world's first. This was followed by another in Kyoto in 1893. These Imperial Universities provided Japan's dedicated bureaucrats and the skilled manpower for the government to nurture its elite managers to run the government-owned new factories. Many new private and public schools and colleges of technology emerged to provide training in commerce and banking practices, international law (English commercial) and English language. These institutions became Japan's major universities and polytechnics in the early 1920s, namely ones such as Keiô, Hitotsubashi, Waseda and Chûô (Sugiyama and Mizuta 1988). These schools and colleges provided opportunities for acquiring expertise in new skills which the traditional apprenticeship based on on-the-job training in the commercial houses could not support.

Government was the prime force in the movement towards industrialization, as commercial capital was incapable of the huge investment in advanced technology required to establish modern industrial production. At about the time of the Meiji Restoration, Japan's GNP per capita was, according to one estimate, one-quarter of that of the UK, and one-third of that of the USA (Minami 1994). In order to alleviate the heavy financial burden, the government sold off many of its commercial enterprises at extremely low prices to private businesses which had established close relationships with government ministers from the late 1870s. The system of limited liabilities based on stocks had been introduced early in the Meiji period (1868–1912), but became established when the new textile firms, capitalized through share issues, began to succeed in the early 1880s (Nihon Sangyô Kunren Kyôkai 1971). By the beginning of the 1890s, the Japanese economy had reached what W. W. Rostow described as the 'take-off' stage of industrialization (Rostow 1960). Greatest development took place first in the light industries centred on textile factories. The two wars, in 1894–5 and in 1904–5 stimulated the development of industry. It was, however, World War I which consolidated Japan's industrial basis by the development of engineering and chemical industries. The industrial production indices rose from 26.3 in 1890 to 93.8 in 1899, 100 in 1900, 158.3 in 1909 and 237 by the end of World War I (Shibagaki 1965).

EMERGENCE OF THE *ZAIBATSU*

Another important development in the first two decades of the twentieth century was the formation of four major business conglomerates known as *zaibatsu* (Mitsui, Mitsubishi, Sumitomo and Yasuda), each controlled by a holding company owned by the family based on kinship (Morikawa 1978). The *zaibatsu* came to dominate Japanese industry in the subsequent decades before World War II. Of these, Mitsui and Sumitomo had their roots back in the seventeenth century, and had become large commercial businesses where the organization was managed by employee managers trained through apprenticeship and on-the-job training. The other two were of more recent origin. Mitsubishi was founded by Yatarô Iwasaki (1834–85), in the early decade of the Meiji period as a shipping company (Mishima 1979), and Yasuda as a bank. Japan's industrialization progressed further in the 1920s and 1930s, and the four major *zaibatsu* were joined by six minor houses of Nomura (securities), Asano (chemicals), Ôkura (mining), Furukawa (mining), Ayukawa (Nissan Motors), and Nakajima (heavy engineering including aircraft) (Morikawa 1978; Okumura 1991). The ten *zaibatsu* accounted for 35.2 per cent of the total paid-up corporate capital of Japan by the end of World War II (Okumura 1991).

With the development of heavy engineering and chemical industries in the 1930s, the ownership of major companies tended to be concentrated in the *zaibatsu* groups, though their businesses were managed by employee managers. For example, the Mitsui Group, the largest of the four major *zaibatsu*, headed by the Mitsui Gomei KK, the group's holding company jointly owned by eleven Mitsui family members, held a large proportion of the shares of the seventy-five major group companies, in banking, insurance, general trading and other wide-ranging sectors. Of these seventy-five companies six designated companies, in general trading, mining, chemicals, shipbuilding, coal mining/shipping and electrical, acted as the holding companies for a further 212 companies below them. This hierarchical relationship spread downwards into subcontractors to create a vast pyramidal structure (*keiretsu*) (Okumura 1991).

The control exercised by the holding company over its subsidiaries and affiliated companies through shareholding was mirrored by a network of directorships. For example, the four representative directors of the Mitsui Gomei KK who had been internally promoted to their executive positions, held between them directorships of thirteen other first-tier companies (Okumura 1991).

Another feature which foreshadowed the post-war characteristics of the Japanese industrial structure was the practice of cross-shareholding among the first-tier member companies. This developed with the release of part of the shares of the holding companies in the 1930s. One of the reasons was undoubtedly to prevent the dilution of the control by the owning family through keeping as many of the shares, released in the open stock market, in the group. But the scale of the cross-holding of shares was not as widespread before World War II as has become the practice in the post-war period.

With such a rapid growth of large firms, the employment of graduates as managers began relatively early in Japan (Morikawa 1978). According to Aonuma's study of large companies and owner/executives, the proportion of owner or shareholder/executives in 1936 was 15 per cent, whilst the backgrounds of the remaining employee/executives were 21.8 per cent through internal promotions, 27.6 per cent from member companies, 10.2 per cent from outside and 25 per cent unknown (Okazaki-Ward 1993). Thus promotional routes for the pre-war top executives in large Japanese companies were fairly heterogeneous, and inter-firm mobility was relatively high. Further, the employee top executives earned high salaries (Prejidento 1989).[1]

Two national employers' associations, *Nihon Keizai Renmei* and *Zensanren*, the former performing economic functions and the latter dealing with labour problems, were co-ordinated and controlled by informal circles formed at the *Nihon Kôgyô Kurabu* or Japan Industrial Club in Tokyo, created in 1917, as the meeting place of the business elite (Okochi, Karsh and Levine, 1973). Politically, the Mitsui *Zaibatsu* was seen to be close to the Liberal Party/*Seiyûkai*, whilst the Mitsubishi *Zaibatsu* to the Progressive Party/*Kenseikai*, though mostly as the providers of the political funds (Morikawa 1978). On the political front, the civilian government, with parliamentary support, succeeded briefly in checking the advance of the military influence in the diet, producing what has become known as the period of 'Taishô democracy', which culminated in universal male suffrage in 1925. It was, however, soon engulfed in the tidal wave of militaristic expansionism which eventually led to World War II.

NOTE

1 A comparison of the ratio of president's pay to that of newly recruited graduate (after tax) below shows that the pre-war difference was considerable: pre-1941 – 100.0 times; 1972 – 10.4 times; 1986 – 8.5 times (Prejidento, February 1988, 260–3).

Chapter 2

Post-war economic and business development

'The Asian phoenix' rising out of the ashes.

(G. Bownas and D. Dickinson, *The Asian Phoenix*)

KEY ISSUES

The main aim of this chapter is to delineate the development of the Japanese economy and business, with a brief description of social and political changes which accompanied it during the period from 1945 to the early 1990s. The period is divided into sub-periods of 1945–58, 1958–73, 1973–80 and 1980–90 which are marked by the clear changes in Japan's economic fortunes, though taken as a whole, it was a period of continuous growth. The chapter provides the explanation as to how the Japanese business groupings, which distinguish the post-war Japanese form of corporate organizations, have been formed. The last part of this chapter examines the grave problems the Japanese business faces in the longest post-war recession in the 1990s, and, in particular, the new issues of corporate governance confronting the Japanese corporate leaders in the mid-1990s.

THE PERIOD 1945 TO 1958

The defeat in World War II left Japan devastated, socially, industrially and economically. The surrender to the Allies in 1945 marked the second major discontinuity for Japan in the modern period. Under the American occupation, a programme of fundamental reforms was introduced to demilitarize and democratize Japan, affecting agricultural land ownership, education, civil, family and industrial relations laws and the political system. The new constitution guaranteed equal rights of all people, and the sovereignty was vested in the people. The highest power was vested in the two-chamber parliament elected by universal suffrage, to which the cabinet, elected from the majority party in parliament was accountable. The policy of non-billigerence was enshrined in the constitution.

Another important measure taken by the Allied forces was the dissolution of the *zaibatsu*, family-owned and other holding companies in order to aid the deconcentration and democratization of the economy. Also the use of the names of the *zaibatsu* families was forbidden. Altogether eighty-three companies, including the major *zaibatsu* holding companies, were targeted for dissolution and the shares held by·them were released on to the market. The resultant dispersal of shares were initially distributed as follows: 38.5 per cent to employees, 27.7 per cent to the general public, and 23.3 per cent to securities companies. However, the purchases were largely backed by the subsidiary companies within each of the former *zaibatsu* group to ensure that their shares did not fall into hostile hands (Okumura 1991).

Many large companies belonging to the *zaibatsu* were broken up by the occupation forces and lost their identity. One curious omission from the target of the deconcentration measures, however, was their banks, who held a large proportion of the shares of their group companies. It was considered too risky by the US occupation forces to target them for deconcentration at a time of financial disruption. For this reason, banks were able to play an important role in the formation of business groupings, the *kigyô shûdan*, which characterizes the forms of Japanese industrial organization in the post-war Japan, along the line of the old combines when the occupation ended.

Another notable measure related to the deconcentration and dissolution of the *zaibatsu*, was the purging of executives in the major companies. In addition to the heads of the fifty-six families from ten *zaibatsu* groups who were banned from holding any public positions, about 2,200 top executives in 250 major companies were deprived of their appointments and prohibited from obtaining executive positions (Hazama 1963). This led to a complete change of personnel at the top of the Japanese business world which had far-reaching implications for the reconstitution of Japanese business leaders. The vacancies created at the top of the leading companies were filled by younger managers from middle-management positions from within, or executives of third-level companies. This is reflected in the Aonuma's 1950 sample which shows that the executives promoted internally accounted for 50.4 per cent of the total whereas those from other member companies accounted for 37.2 per cent (Aonuma 1965). Equally, there was a significant fall in the age of directors. Almost 90 per cent of these executives were graduates and one-third of them had science/technology backgrounds (Aonuma in Okazaki-Ward 1993). Although these young executives were inexperienced, they were, however, ready to introduce new technologies, to aggressively compete, and were keen to embrace new management techniques to improve their performance.

Formation of the key economic organizations

The period between 1946 and 1949 saw the establishment of the four key economic organizations which were to represent the business world of Japan (*zaikai*) in its relations with government, labour, the mass media and foreign countries. They were *Keizai Dantai Rengôkai* (the Federation of Economic Organizations, *Keidanren* for short), *Keizai Dôyûkai* (the Association of Corporate Executives) both established in 1946, *Nihon Keieisha Dantai Renmei* (the Japan Federation of Employers' Associations, *Nikkeiren* for short) established in 1948, and *Nihon Shôkô Kaigisho* (the Japan Chamber of Commerce and Industry, or JCCI, *Nisshô* for short) the origin of which goes back to 1922. Though differing in their objectives and often in their opinions on political and economic matters, they came together to issue joint statements to express the agreed and shared viewpoint of the business world. While *Keidanren* represents the voice of large businesses, the views of small and medium enterprises are represented by *Nisshô*. The *Nikkeiren* serves as the employers' counterpart to trade unions, while *Keizai Dôyûkai*, whose members are individual executives rather than businesses, aims to promote progress, stability and provide opportunity for the development of its members. The four organizations have run and carry out extensive surveys, publish reports and make proposals aimed at benefiting the national economy (Okazaki-Ward 1993). The leaders of these organizations have been and are chairmen and presidents of Japan's major corporations.

Korean War, 1950 to 1951

The Korean War, 1950–1, proved to be the powerful lifeline that Japan needed for economic recovery. The effect of an increase in world trade stimulated by the war on the Japanese economy was 'nothing short of prodigious' (Nakamura 1981). Exports grew by a factor of 2.7, and production increased by nearly 70 per cent between 1949 and 1951 (Nakamura 1981). There was also a remarkable rise in corporate rates of return on gross capital employed, due to the rise in prices that accompanied the increases in production. Another important effect of this boom was that it prompted a vigorous expansion in investment in plant and equipment. But the most important factor for the Japanese economy was the foreign exchange income derived from the expenditure of the US army and military personnel engaged in the Korean War – special procurement – which raised the ceiling on the nation's balance of payments at a single stroke, enabling a doubling of imports and hence doubling the scale of industrial production (Nakamura 1981).

The industrial reconstruction policies of 1951 and 1952 were centred on 'capital accumulation', measures which became the prototype for Japan's post-war industrial policies. These measures included the establishment of the Japan Development Bank to supply low-interest loans to key industries, and the Export–Import Bank to finance exporting firms; the lowering of corporate tax burdens; the imposition of a foreign exchange allocation system that virtually protected domestic industry; and the importation of advanced foreign technologies to accompany the increase in plant and equipment investment (Nakamura 1981).

Technological development is one reason for Japan's fast post-war growth, one that enabled Japan to catch up with the West in the immediate period after World War II, during which a considerable technological gap had developed between Japan and the West. The government played a crucial role during the first twenty years after the war in ensuring the importation of critical technology. MITI (the Ministry of International Trade and Industry), created in 1949 and using the power to approve or reject the purchase of foreign inventions by Japanese companies, ensured that any contract for technology imports was one that was consistent with MITI's plan for the development of Japanese industry. MITI offices were set up around the world to scan for new technological advances in order to provide the requisite information to Japanese firms. MITI also stood as referee to ensure that the price paid in royalties, contract length or restrictions such as export limits was not too high for the purchasing companies. Once the technology contract was formalized, MITI ensured that funds were directed to bring that technology on stream. Between 1951 and 1970 a total of over 13,000 cases of technological contracts were recorded, averaging 650 per year, and thereafter rising to about 2,000 per year into the 1980s (Abegglen and Stalk 1985).

Already in 1950, the Ministry of Finance and the Bank of Japan established a measure whereby fiscal surpluses would be channelled back through commercial banks and other financial institutions to private businesses in terms of providing substantial loans on exceptionally favourable terms, thereby strengthening the wealth-creation sector of the economy. This re-established the pre-war links between the banks and the group member firms and led to the reformation of business groupings. The role played by the banks in the implementation of the 'capital accumulation' measures was most influential. Their influence, however, also led to the so-called over-loan phenomenon, whereby increases in commercial bank lending exceeded increases in deposits. The Bank of Japan stood as guarantor, thereby strengthening the bank's control over the city banks, a particular feature of post-war Japanese industrial policy.

Capital financing by debt dominated Japanese business for the next thirty years, and institutionalized the system of the 'main bank' whereby the position of the group bank became a powerful influence on the activities of the client corporations.

With the signing of the peace treaty in September 1951 and the security pact in 1952, Japan regained its independence while remaining unarmed, except for self-defence, and its security guaranteed by the US nuclear umbrella. Thus, at the second turning point in its modern history, Japan dropped the second half of the Meiji Restoration slogan, 'rich country, strong army' (*fukoku kyôhei*) and resolved to pursue the first half of the slogan single-mindedly in order to gain industrial dominance.

Important in this respect was the reformation in 1952 of the business groupings along the lines of the pre-war *zaibatsu* membership by Mitsubishi, Mitsui and Sumitomo. The move was triggered by the threat of takeover of some of the member companies through the outflow of their shares to non-group owners. This galvanized the member companies, until then broken up, and fragmented, during the occupation, into a series of actions that affirmed their solidarity under their old flagship names which they were again allowed to use. The group banks arranged to buy up the erstwhile shares and allocated them to the other member companies for safe keeping. In order to facilitate such share acquisitions, strong pressures were brought to bear upon the government through *keidanren* in 1953 to revise Clause Ten of the post-war Anti-Monopoly Law. By this revision, the restrictions on the corporate holding of shares of other companies were practically removed. The original limit of 5 per cent imposed on any banks' holding of shares of any single company was increased to 10 per cent, preparing the ground for an increase in cross-holding of shares by the member companies of the pre-*zaibatsu* groupings. This was consolidated soon after when many companies increased their capital base through the equity market.

The formation of the Presidents' Clubs (*Shachôkai*) by the presidents of the major firms of each of the groups as a forum for co-ordinated actions and discussion of general group policies, also took place around this time (Okumura 1991). In those early days, the role of such a club as a forum for the members to discuss, formulate and enforce group policies, became a significant influence on corporate strategy.

Around the same time, companies which were part of the minor *zaibatsu* which had lacked a group bank, began to form new horizontal business groupings with the major city banks such as Fuji (the previous Yasuda Bank which did not have secondary sector firms under its umbrella in the pre-war time), Daiichi (before its merger with Kangyô) and Sanwa Banks, through loans and cross-holding of shares. In 1958, 22.4 per cent of the total shares issued were held by financial institutions, 15.8 per cent by incorporated enterprises, 49.1 per cent by individual investors, 6.6 per cent by investment trusts and 4.4 per cent by the securities (Okumura 1991).

The period 1952 to 1958 marks the first stage of concentration of shares into business groupings through cross-shareholding, for the purpose of security, and as a result, saw the establishment of the six major business groupings (the horizontal *kigyô shûdan*) of Mitsubishi, Mitsui, Sumitomo, Fuji, Daiichi and Sanwa. Each were a group of two dozen or more large companies who chose to identify themselves as members of the same business grouping either out of tradition or for expediency. The individual companies were no longer controlled by the holding company, but independent entities ranged around the group bank which met their primary capital needs. These business groupings have come to dominate the Japanese industrial landscape ever since.

Politics and economics

In 1955 the two existing conservative political parties amalgamated to create the Liberal Democratic Party (LDP) which was to stay in power for the next thirty-eight years, providing a stable, pro-business political environment for economic growth. It also prepared the ground for the formation of an alliance among the political, business and bureaucratic leaders, the 'iron triangle', which comprised the ruling elite of Japan.

During the five-year period between 1955 and 1960, the GNP grew at the real rate of 9.1 per cent per year and in 1956 the then Prime Minister, Nobusuke Kishi, was able to proclaim economic recovery by saying that 'it is no longer the post-war economy' (Nakamura 1981). By 1958 Japan's industrial output was back to the pre-war level (Clark 1979).

New management ideas

In 1958, two important publications on management significantly influenced thinking. One was a monograph by James Abegglen entitled *The Japanese Factory* in which he identified, as a major difference from American companies, the existence of specific employment practices and a system of wage determination and promotion by means of seniority through a 'lifelong commitment' between the employees and their companies. When the book was translated into Japanese the term became *shûshin koyô* which was re-translated back into English as 'lifetime employment' and passed into the Japanese employment management vocabulary. The other was an introductory book on management by Fujiyoshi Sakamura which, being written in relatively easy and jargon-free style, captured the imagination of practising managers (Nihon Sangyô Kunren Kyôkai 1971). These two books started a boom in the introduction and application of American management techniques.

Prior to this time, from 1949, three management training courses, the CCS course for top executives, organized and taught by the Civil Communication Section of the Allied Headquarters, the MTP (Management Training Programme) for middle management and the TWI (Training Within Industry) for supervisory-level personnel, had been introduced by the American forces. These were administered by *Nikkeiren* and developed and taught by the *Nihon Sangyô Kunren Kyôkai* (Japan Industrial and Vocational Training Association: JIVTA for short), created for that purpose in 1955. In the same year *Nihon Seisansei Honbu* (the Japan Productivity Centre, JPC) was established through aid funds to help improve the productivity of Japanese industry. JPC sent seventeen industrial missions to the USA during the first year alone, and the number increased each year so that by 1959 there were over one hundred missions organized. Seeing the technologically advanced production facilities in operation in the United States greatly stimulated Japanese managers to improve their production installations and management, and prepared the ground for the keen introduction of American management techniques. In 1958, the JPC also began the now famous annual top executive management seminars (JIVTA 1971). Many new management techniques were introduced from the US and eagerly seized upon by Japanese managers trying to improve their performance. Some of them, such as the use of 'job descriptions', were later discarded because they were found to be incompatible with the current Japanese practices. At the end of this period, the Japanese economy was poised for a decade and a half of rapid expansion which took the rest of the world by surprise.

THE PERIOD 1958 TO 1973

Introduction

This period can be labelled as the time of the Japanese 'economic miracle', when the economy grew at a phenomenal rate. Japan was made a member of the OECD, and its GNP in dollar terms put it in third place after the US and the USSR in 1968. Consolidation of the Japanese business groupings occurred so that by the end of the period all the features of Japanese 'corporatist capitalism', which came to distinguish Japanese corporate practices from those of the US and the UK, were in place. The standard of living rose, as did the educational and health standard of the young people. However, towards the end of this era, the problem of pollution caused by rapid industrialization was a serious social issue. The period of high economic growth was brought to an end by the first oil crisis in 1973.

The economy

In 1960 the Prime Minister, Hayato Ikeda, unveiled the now famous 'Income Doubling Plan' aimed at increasing the national income two-fold within the following decade. There was a boom in capital investment in 1960 and 1961 to support the growth. The GNP grew at an average real annual rate of 10.9 per cent during the decade and the Ikeda plan was fulfilled by 1967 (Nakamura 1981; Okochi, Karsh and Levine 1973). Japan was admitted formally into the OECD and GATT in the first half of the 1960s. The growth was achieved through an improvement in the trade balance. Further, certain measures to liberalize the Japanese market also followed Japan's membership of OECD in 1964. In 1968, one hundred years after the Meiji Restoration, Japan's GDP was the second largest, after the USA, in the non-communist world.

Rise in living standards and education

This period was, on the whole, one of a sustained rise in wages and living standards. The great boom in capital investment of 1960–1 produced an unprecedented growth which continued throughout the decade, except for a short period in 1964–5. Wages increased by 8.7 per cent in 1960, and jumped in 1961 by 13.8 per cent as a result of a successful 'spring offensive', the annual ritual of wage negotiation mounted by the labour unions (Nakamura 1981). The achievement of large increases in pay throughout the 1960s imbued the people with the notion that rapid growth, accompanied by rising incomes and living standards, had come to stay. The Japanese economy was locked into a virtuous circle of growth and full employment.

With rising income, the lifestyle of the Japanese people became more Westernized. Moreover, the rapid urbanization accompanying the expansion of industry, the ownership of telephones, cars, air-conditioning and colour television sets expanded enormously during the decade. The diet of the people shifted from the traditional rice-based fare to a protein- and fat-rich diet. Noticeably the health and physique of children began to improve markedly. There were also more children staying on for a further three years of secondary education (82 per cent), and by 1970 a larger proportion of 18-year-olds (24 per cent) were going on to higher education, helped by an expansion of the tertiary sector in the latter part of the 1960s (Aso 1983). The four-fold rise in per capita income between 1961 and 1970 promoted the investment in the education of the next generation. Advances in technology required a larger number of graduates in science and technological subjects and the demand was met by an increase in the number of universities and faculties in the private sector. Major firms began taking on large numbers of male university graduates into their management cadre to groom them for future management roles. Higher education increasingly came to be seen as the means for securing a future in a large company. Competition for entry into the prestigious universities began to heat up.

Changes in the structure of business groupings

The expanding economy of the late 1950s and early 1960s offered an increased opportunity for the growth of new industries such as synthetic fibres, petrochemicals, home electrical appliances and motor cars, based on new technology. There was a need for a massive capital investment but the huge appetite of big companies for capital could not be satisfied by their group financial institutions. Other financing channels such as banks and insurance companies outside the groupings, as well as foreign capital in the form of impact and tied loans, were explored. The 'main bank' system was strengthened to ensure the premium position of influence of the group bank over the borrower against other banks. However, financing by debt was expensive, so the companies turned to the stock market through the issues of large-scale stocks, stimulating the rapid growth of investment trusts in the first half of the 1960s. As cross-holding became a barrier to large-scale share issues, the solidarity of the *kigyô shûdan* was relaxed to cope with the capital expansion, resulting in the lowering of the level of the cross-holding of shares among the member companies of the business groupings. The rapid change in the industrial structure caused by the introduction of new industries also resulted in intra-group competition within the ex-*zaibatsu* groups. Furthermore, some of the large companies attempted to become independent from the loosely formed newer, bank-centred groupings. A re-grouping of companies in the *kigyô shûdan* took place. The equity market remained very active until 1964, when there followed a sudden crash in stock prices. The result was that securities companies, in particular Yamaichi Securities, as well as the investment trusts, went to the wall, and the economy went into sudden recession.

The government stepped in to freeze the shares off-loaded onto the market through falling stock prices which amounted to 5.1 per cent of all shares issued by those companies listed on the first section of the Japanese Stock Exchanges in 1965 (Okumura 1991). This action halted the prices falling further, and also stopped the shares of the blue-chip companies, up to 10 per cent of the total shares on the market, being bought up by the foreign companies, thus preventing the possibility of these premier companies being taken over by the foreign interests. These frozen shares were subsequently released between 1967 and 1971, by which time the economy was well on course for further expansion. The shares were bought up primarily by the group companies, led by the banks, to prevent them going outside the groupings. For example, the proportion of the shares bought by thirteen city banks accounted for 20.6 per cent of the total shares released. Particularly notable was the substantial acquisition of shares by the Fuji Bank, amounting to 4 per cent of the total, followed by Sumitomo (2.9 per cent), Mitsubishi (2.8 per cent) and Sanwa (2.4 per cent) banks. At the same time, a mutual acquisition of the shares by member companies occurred, particularly, if not exclusively, amongst the Fuyô (Fuji Bank), Daiichi and Sanwa business groupings where cross-holding of shares between individual companies was not customary until then as relationships had remained loose (Okumura 1991). Also notable was the large proportion (14.1 per cent) of the released shares acquired by the five major life insurance companies. Before the crash, the life insurance companies had become the top shareholders of many of the blue-chip companies. The government pressed them to maintain their position so as to prevent too high a concentration of the shares in the hands of the banks (Okumura 1991). As a result, the shares held by incorporated companies including banks as the proportion of the total shares issued had increased once again, from 48.7 per cent in 1967 to 51.7 per cent in 1968, and to 56.2 per cent in 1971, thus increasing the level of cross-holding of shares by the member companies. The short and sharp recession of 1964–5 can be seen to have triggered the second round of concentration of shareholding into the hands of incorporated enterprises and the consolidation of key business groupings through heightened cross-shareholding. The stock price crash also triggered a new wave of restructuring in industries, prompting amalgamation and rationalization of companies.

Another rationale for the cross-holding of shares which came into prominence in the late 1960s was the *antei kabunushi kôsaku* (stable shareholder creation manoeuvring) in order to prevent takeovers, particularly by foreign multinationals. The liberalization of capital was introduced in five steps between 1967 and 1973 by which time practically all restrictions had gone. Most anxious about the possible foreign share participation and particularly hostile acquisition was the motor industry which began to push the *antei kabunushi kôsaku* strongly. Toyota, for example, who began the process in 1967 managed to stabilize in stages, 70 per cent of its total shares, by first allocating them to banks and insurance companies of the Mitsui group, then to other major companies of the group, and extending the allocation to the major steel suppliers and association of subcontractors who could be relied on not selling them. By this action it declared its affiliation to the Mitsui group. Nissan, Hino and Matsuda followed suit with other groups (Okumura 1991). The released frozen shares mentioned earlier were also subjected to similar operations to ensure their stable ownership. Alerted to the danger of takeover, the car companies then began acquiring the shares of their major suppliers to ensure that they would not fall into the hands of their competitors, domestic or foreign, consolidating the vertical *keiretsu* (same group) relationships between the big firm at the top and a pyramid of suppliers below. The fear of takeover spread to the second-tier companies, and there was a scramble for the *antei kabunushi kôsaku* among them, driving up the share prices, which made it attractive for corporate shareholders to hold such shares. This was facilitated by the revision of the Securities Trading Law, making share trading on the open market easier. While an increased desire by foreign multinationals to enter the Japanese stock market seems obvious by the rise in the proportion of the total shares they held from 1968 (see Table 2.1), their progress was somewhat slow, never rising beyond 3.6 per cent, and no doubt impeded by the *antei kabunushi kôsaku*.

Between 1958 and 1973, the pattern of shareholding by different sectors of shareholders changed. The shares held by individual shareholders, which was about half the total shareholding in 1958, fell to less than one-third by 1973. With the maturing of the business grouping system in the late 1960s, even the extra large independent firms, like Shin Nittetsu, Hitachi and Toyota, saw the advantages of being part of a large group and began to move under the banner of various business groupings. This was not to say, however, that this trend left no large independent companies standing outside the business groupings, as Honda, Sony and Matsushita have remained outside of the *kigyô shûdan*.

Another important change which occurred toward the end of the 1960s was in the issuing price of shares. The practice of issuing shares at par, dating back to pre-war times, was scrapped and the issuing of shares at market value was introduced. This was promoted by the Ministry of Finance and the industrial elite groups because they felt that the old practice did not work in accordance with market principles. For a company doing well, the amount of fund gained from par-value issues was not only small, at Y100 each, but also the same as those issued by the company performing poorly. The practice of issuing new shares in an open market at market price caught on in the 1970s. In 1968 only 3.6 per cent of shares were issued at market price: that percentage had stabilized at around 70 per cent by the late 1970s (Okumura 1991).

By the end of this period, the practices of corporate cross-shareholding and *antei kabunushi kôsaku*, which were designed to ensure stable mutual shareholding by the business group member companies as well as long-term trading relationships between them, became institutionalized in Japan along with the practice of issuing shares at market price. This meant that many large companies, who had held the shares of other companies for a long time, could expect an increase in the value of their shareholding, manipulated by the above-mentioned practices (Okumura 1991). These practices, as part of an interrelated set of Japanese business

Table 2.1 Proportions of shares held by different ownership groups (per cent)

	A	B	C	D	E	F	G
1949	2.8	9.9	—	12.6	5.6	69.1	—
1950	3.1	12.6	—	11.9	11.0	61.3	—
1951	1.8	13.0	5.2	9.2	13.8	57.0	—
1952	1.0	15.8	6.0	8.4	11.8	55.8	1.2
1953	0.7	16.3	6.7	7.3	13.5	53.9	1.1
1954	0.5	16.7	7.0	7.1	13.0	54.0	1.7
1955	0.4	19.5	4.1	7.9	13.2	53.1	1.8
1956	0.3	21.7	3.9	7.1	15.7	49.9	1.5
1957	0.2	21.4	4.7	5.7	16.3	50.1	1.5
1958	0.3	22.4	6.6	4.4	15.8	49.1	1.5
1959	0.2	21.7	7.6	3.7	17.5	47.8	1.5
1960	0.2	23.1	7.5	3.7	17.8	46.3	1.4
1961	0.2	21.4	8.6	2.8	18.7	46.7	1.7
1962	0.2	21.5	9.2	2.5	17.7	47.1	1.8
1963	0.2	21.4	9.5	2.2	17.9	46.7	2.1
1964	0.2	21.6	7.5	4.4	18.4	45.6	1.9
1965	0.2	23.4	5.6	5.8	18.4	44.8	1.8
1966	0.2	26.1	3.7	5.4	18.6	44.1	1.9
1967	0.3	28.2	2.4	4.4	20.5	42.3	1.9
1968	0.3	30.3	1.7	2.1	21.4	41.9	2.3
1969	0.3	30.7	1.2	1.4	22.0	41.1	3.3
1970	0.3	30.9	1.4	1.2	23.1	39.9	3.2
1971	0.2	32.6	1.3	1.5	23.6	37.2	3.6
1972	0.2	33.8	1.3	1.8	26.6	32.7	3.5
1973	0.2	33.9	1.2	1.5	27.5	32.7	3.0
1974	0.2	33.9	1.6	1.3	27.1	33.4	2.5
1975	0.2	34.5	1.6	1.4	26.3	33.5	2.6
1976	0.2	35.1	1.4	1.4	26.5	32.9	2.6
1977	0.2	35.9	2.0	1.5	26.1	32.0	2.3
1978	0.2	36.6	2.2	1.8	26.2	30.8	2.1
1979	0.2	36.9	1.9	2.0	26.1	30.4	2.5
1980	0.2	37.3	1.5	1.7	26.0	29.2	4.0
1981	0.2	37.3	1.3	1.7	26.3	28.4	4.6
1982	0.2	37.7	1.2	1.8	26.0	28.0	5.1
1983	0.2	38.0	1.0	1.9	25.9	26.8	6.3
1984	0.2	38.5	1.1	1.9	25.9	26.3	6.1
1985	0.8	40.9	1.3	2.0	24.1	25.2	5.7
1986	0.9	41.7	1.8	2.2	24.5	23.9	4.7
1987	0.8	42.2	2.4	2.5	24.9	23.6	3.6
1988	0.7	42.5	3.1	2.5	24.9	22.4	4.0
1989	0.7	42.3	3.7	2.0	24.8	22.6	3.9

Source: Okumura 1991
Note: A Government and public bodies; B banks and other lesser investment trusts;
C investment trusts; D securities; E incorporated companies; F private investors;
G foreign investors

practices were termed by Okumura 'corporatist capitalism' (Okumura 1991) as distinct from market capitalism practised in the West. This 'corporatist capitalism' has remained the feature of the Japanese economy throughout post-war Japan.

The 'corporatist' practices enabled Japanese corporations to be oriented to long-term horizons in their investment planning, to concentrate on expansion of market share for their product rather than on short-term profit, and to give precedence to management of employees rather than shareholder interests. This employee-oriented approach of the Japanese to management has been described as *Jinpon-shugi* (Human-capitalism) (Itami 1990a). Each business grouping was often likened to a large convoy (*gosô sendan*), finding security in moving as a mass (Okumura 1991).

Environmental pollution

A serious negative effect of the rapid economic growth throughout the 1960s and into the early 1970s was the wide-ranging pollution caused in the environment because of the rapid development of chemical and heavy industries and the spread of the automobile. As serious cases of pollution and its effect on the populace were brought to light throughout the 1960s, pollution became a grave social issue. The government established in 1967 that the burden of compensation for the losses incurred would be borne by the polluting companies and a series of laws for prevention of air, water and noise pollution were passed. However, a firm stand by the government was not taken until 1970 when its hitherto stated goal favouring industrial development was revised. The Environment Agency was inaugurated in the following year to enforce preventive regulations and to monitor the effects of industry on the environment. Behind this change of stance towards supporting industry was a shift in public opinion which no longer unanimously endorsed a high rate of economic growth at the cost to the environment. However, irrespective of public opinion, this high rate of economic growth was brought to a halt by the economic crisis of 1973.

THE PERIOD 1973 TO 1980

Introduction

The first oil crisis of 1973 triggered a round of rationalization, and promoted a change in the industrial structure of the country prompting the growth of the 'knowledge-intensive' industries and downgrading those dependent on imported oil. The economy settled into a stable growth in the second half of the decade which the second oil crisis of 1979 did not dampen. However, Japan's steady increase of trade surpluses brought it into conflict with the nations of the West.

Turbulence

The 1970s proved to be a decade of turbulence. The first sign of trouble was the yen revaluation which came to be known as the 'Nixon shock'. The exchange rate for the yen had been fixed at Y360 to the dollar since 1949. However, Japan's international competitiveness had grown dramatically, and as it accumulated trade surpluses since 1967, the yen came to be regarded as undervalued. The initial fears, following the flotation of the yen in 1971, that the Japanese economy would be damaged turned out to be somewhat exaggerated. In the following year, the Tanaka cabinet's 'Plan for Rebuilding the Japanese Archipelago', caused land prices to soar, helped by a high level of corporate retained surpluses available for speculative investment in land. The resultant inflation was, however, soon brought to heel by the government's tight money policy. Then came the first 'oil crisis' in October 1973. The price increases were a stunning blow to all countries dependent on Middle Eastern oil, and particularly hard on Japan, dependent on imported crude oil for three-quarters of its primary energy resources. The repercussions of the price rise in crude oil for the economy were far reaching. Corporate profits fell dramatically due to declining demand and rising prices. Costs rose even higher because of a large increase in wages to counter the effects of inflation. Mining and manufacturing declined by 19 per cent between the end of 1973 to the first quarter of 1975, the biggest such fall in post-war history. The severest blow fell on the chemical and heavy industries immediately, followed by shipbuilding, steel and later textiles. Only the strongly export-competitive industries such as the automobile industry and certain industries such as food products, remained relatively unaffected. Inventory rose and resulted in business plant and operation ratios falling by about 25 per cent in 1975 as compared with the beginning of 1973. The severity of the recession brought the period of high growth of the previous twenty years to an end. Economic growth slowed down to 2 per cent in 1975. In order to cope with the recession, 'scale-down' (genryô keiei) policies were adopted by firms (Nakamura 1981).

There were three categories of activities that came under the 'scale-down' operation. The first was a reduction in the number of employees and in labour costs. The second related to finance, namely cost – paring down the interest burden. The third was the cutting of cost in all remaining areas.

The financial cutback concerned the scale of borrowing and the level of interest rates. Given the Japanese firms' high gearing ratio (the equity capital ratio was 13.9 per cent in 1975) (Nakamura 1981) and the tight money policy of the government which lasted until 1975, the task was quite enormous. The effort to reduce the borrowing burden did not bear fruit until the interest rate came down by stages between 1977 and 1978 when it reached 6.09 per cent (Nakamura 1981).

Labour rationalization was inevitable given that most firms had to reduce the scale of production because of the reduction in energy supplies. The first to be axed were the part-time workers. Thereafter, the situation was more difficult to handle because of the 'lifetime' employment practice. In order to preserve good labour–management relations, firms had to avoid large, sweeping cutbacks in their workforce. Every imaginable device available to reduce the burden of labour cost within the constraints of 'lifetime' employment was used. These included reductions in overtime, non-renewal of contracts for non-core employees, a cutback or a stopping in recruitment, secondment and transfer to other companies, cuts in the pay and bonuses of top executives and middle management, a call for voluntary retirement, reductions in dividend distribution, and the sale of assets. Particularly hard hit were large firms in the manufacturing sector, where the labour force was reduced by more than 700,000 between 1973 and 1978 (Nakamura 1981). In shipbuilding alone, which had expanded quickly in the 1960s, employment was cut from 200,000 to 60,000 in the same period (Shimada 1994). Although the government set up an employment adjustment grant scheme to avert large scale redundancies in those industries worst hit by the crisis as much to avoid social unrest, the worst of the manpower adjustment was essentially borne by the blue-collar workers. One key to the success of bringing down labour cost was the co-operation of the enterprise labour unions in moderating the rates of wage increases in the annual 'spring offensive', which had the additional positive impact of keeping down inflationary pressures. The wage increase rate plummeted from 33 per cent in 1974 to 5.9 per cent in 1978 (Nakamura 1981). There was a considerable shift in the number of people employed from the secondary sector to the tertiary sector of the economy, particularly in wholesale and retail, finance and insurance. The unemployment rate rose above the critical 2 per cent point.

The expansion of the tertiary sector was marked during the 1970s, seizing new opportunities for growth afforded by the rapid change in the domestic lifestyle of the Japanese which had taken another turn towards Westernization. Also the inter-regional equalization of incomes ensured homogeneity of consumption patterns throughout the country. Large supermarket chains mushroomed. New business opportunities in the service industry, such as in dining-out, were created. The tertiary sector enjoyed overall expansion and new growth in areas where before there had been little activity. In this way, the tertiary sector absorbed many of the people who were displaced from the secondary sector.

Thirdly, examples of other cutbacks were inventory reductions, suppression of plant and equipment investment except where it was unavoidable, economizing in fuel and raw materials in every field, the adoption of electronics devices, numerically controlled (NC) machine tools and robots to increase automation. The concerted effort of government, unions and industry bore fruit and by the end of 1978, profit rates showed clear signs of recovery.

However, the oil crisis came as an enormous shock to the Japanese economy which had experienced rapid expansion during the 1960s and in the early 1970s primarily in the petrochemical and in the high energy-consuming steel and aluminium industry, fuelled by cheap imported oil. A strenuous effort was made to reduce energy consumption, with the result that the level of consumption was lower in 1978 than in 1973, and the volume of oil import in the early 1980s remained below the level of 1973. The industrial structure underwent a transformation, from being centred on heavy, long, large, thick and basic products to miniature, more knowledge-intensive, high-technology and high value-added products. The role MITI (Ministry of International Trade and Industry) played in setting the direction of the change by laying down an agenda for industrial development away from the chemical and heavy industries for the coming decade and acting as a facilitator for such development, was important and considerable. In 1971 MITI published a report entitled *The Basic Direction of Trade and Industry in the 1970s*. The report emphasized the importance of developing knowledge-based industries including electronics, computers, semiconductor industries, information services and system engineering, pointing the direction of the future development away from an emphasis on chemical and heavy industries (Minami 1994). Included in this report was support for the development of robots and numerically controlled machines. This report, predating the first oil crisis, became a ready blueprint for the later changes in industrial structure necessitated by the two oil crises. Industrial robots and numerically controlled devices were introduced in large numbers in the latter half of the 1970s in response to the need for labour cost reduction. These machines proved to be immensely significant in the improvement of the quality of Japanese products (Abegglen and Stalk 1985).

Central to this shift was the prominent position that the automobile and electronics industry came to occupy. They featured primarily in exports which began to increase from 1976, strongly supporting economic recovery. Throughout the latter half of the 1970s the real GDP growth rate averaged a stable 5.0 per cent thus ensuring steady growth. Japan's trade surplus averaged US$11 billion (Keizai Kôhô Centre 1982), and the accumulation of trade surpluses, whilst helping to expand the economy, also brought Japan increasingly into conflict with other developed nations, foreshadowing the pattern of trade relations that was to become familiar in the 1980s.

Thus Japan was relatively well prepared to ride out the impact of the second oil crisis of 1979. The price of crude oil jumped from $11 per barrel at the end of 1978 to $30 at the beginning of 1980. The government swiftly introduced a tight fiscal policy at an early stage, successfully curbing domestic price increases, but only long enough so that domestic demand did not stagnate (Nakamura 1981). Once the crisis was over, the Japanese began to invest heavily in the development of new technology, thus making its products competitive in world markets.

THE 1980s

Introduction

The decade saw the internationalization of the Japanese economy, and industry becoming increasingly globalized. Such epithets as the 'economic superpower' were used to describe Japan's influence on the world economy. Japan's continuous accumulation of trade surpluses brought in its wake trade friction with major economies and led to the revaluation of the yen halfway through the decade. Towards the end of the decade, Japan experienced an enormous expansion in asset values which came to be known as the 'bubble'.

Internationalism

In 1981, MITI issued a report called *Trade and Industry Policies for the 1980s* covering a far wider scope than the 1971 report. The 1981 report outlined a requirement for Japan to develop more reliable sources of energy and to become less dependent on oil. It also visualized a decade in which highly sophisticated technology using new materials and systems would develop, reducing reliance on heavy and chemical industries (Minami 1994). In the following year, the Science & Technology Agency declared the year 1981 as 'the first year of the era of Japan's technological independence' (Science & Technology Agency 1982; Abegglen and Stalk 1985), highlighting the importance of self-developed technology through independent and innovative research. The R&D expenditure increased from being 2.35 per cent of the national income in 1980 to 3.54 per cent in 1991 and by more than four-fold in actual amount in dollar terms. This seemingly inconsistency is because of the synergistic effect of the GNP in yen terms doubling and the yen going up in value by 40 per cent against the dollar (Keizai Kôhô Centre 1994).

Only 17 per cent of this sum was borne by government sources, as compared to 43 per cent in the US. Also the balance in trading in technology by Japan by the end of the 1980s, showed an improvement. Japan received 0.8 times as much as it spent on buying technology though rather behind the US, the biggest exporter of technology in the world, which received 2.6 times as much as it had paid (Jackson 1993).

High-quality, mass-produced goods, centred on electronic products and cars were the driving force of the growth of the Japanese economy in the 1980s. Proven first in terms of cost and quality in an extremely competitive domestic market, these commodities were exported in large volumes, earning Japan an ever-expanding annual trade surplus. The Japanese corporations made increasingly larger profits which, in the absence of pressures from the shareholders, were spent on further technological innovation as well as retained as accumulated reserves. However, continuously increasing annual trade surpluses, jumping to $19 billion in 1981 and rising to $55 billion in 1985, also earned Japan accusations from abroad of lacking the will to open its own market to imports to reduce the trade imbalance. Not surprisingly, Japan became further involved in fierce trade frictions with the Western nations that had become its main markets. The Japanese car makers, tired of trade embargoes and 'voluntary' restraint imposed upon their exports, took the initiative by locating their manufacturing facilities first in the US and then in Europe. In 1980, Honda pioneered the Japanese car manufacturing presence in the US. Other major car makers followed. This marked the beginning of the 'globalization' of Japanese industry. The car manufacturers were followed by an increasing number of makers of exported goods, such as videos, cameras, business machines, hi-fi equipment, radios, printing machines, who located their manufacturing facilities in the markets for these goods. In the first half of the 1980s, Japan's annual Direct Overseas Investment increased from $4.7 billion in 1980 to $12.2 billion in 1985 whilst gross domestic product grew at 3.7 per cent annually on average, and the exchange rate for the yen in 1985 was at an annual average of Y238.54 to the dollar (Keizai Kôhô Centre 1990).

During the first five years of the 1980s, basic wages negotiated through *shuntô*, the labour 'spring offensive', rose at an annual average of 5.5 per cent. Further, Japanese consumer tastes were changing, due to an increasing rise in standards of living, turning away from mass-produced products to those which took account of individual expression, as well as acquiring a thirst for luxury goods from abroad. The enhancement of consumer sophistication was also helped by an increase in the number of Japanese tourists, from nearly 4 million in 1980 to 4.9 million in 1985 and to 6.8 million in 1987. The Japanese saw with their own eyes how the people of the USA and Europe lived. Furthermore, more money was spent on education, as over 93 per cent of 15-year-olds were opting for a further three years of secondary education, and those 18-year-olds who were going on for higher education were nearing the 37 per cent mark by 1987 (Keizai Kôhô Centre 1989). There were more than 500 universities and somewhat more junior colleges by the end of the 1980s.

The unrelenting rise of trade surpluses registered by Japan resulted in an agreement to revalue the yen at the meeting of the G5 in September 1985. The yen rose 80 per cent in the following 18 months, to an average of Y168.52 in 1986 and to Y128.15 to the dollar in 1988. The Japanese government released Y2 billion into the domestic economy, centred on home construction, to stimulate domestic demand. Equally, the official discount rate was lowered by progressive steps to 2.5 per cent, by the end of 1986 where it remained until May 1989, a post-war low (Ministry of Finance Study Group 1993). The combined effect of these measures was successful in terms of growth. After an initial dip in economic performance in 1986 when the annual growth was 2.5 per cent, the economy began to grow, led by domestic demand, at an average of 5.1 per cent in the next four years. This was no doubt promulgated by the excessive level of consumer disposable income which was looking for an outlet. Further, manufacturing went through a cost-cutting exercise to maintain the competitiveness of their exported products. The redeployment of labour consequent upon rationalization was made easier by an extensive diversification of business operations in industry.

But the revaluation, designed to reduce Japan's trade surplus, did not produce its desired effect. Japan's annual trade balance remained in the $90 billion region until 1988, falling to $63.6 billion by 1990, by which time the yen had rallied slightly to Y144.79 against the US dollar. This was particularly discomforting for the United States which faced the twin deficit in trade and budget. Its large trade deficit with Japan resulted in open and aggressive pressure on Japan to make its domestic market easier to enter.

Rise of the 'bubble'

The modest growth figures of the second half of the 1980s do not reflect the enormous extent of the asset price expansion that occurred in Japan between 1987 and 1990. This expansion has since become known as the 'bubble', because the rise in asset prices cannot be explained in terms of economic fundamentals. For example, the total price of property assets burgeoned 2.4 times between the end of 1985 and the end of 1990, with the value at the end of 1990 being Y2,389 trillion, representing five times the size of Japan's GNP for that year. In fact, the 1990 year-end total was so enormous that it amounted, in dollar terms, to roughly four times the value of all land values in the US

(Ministry of Finance Study Group 1993). Behind this comparison has also been the appreciation of the yen which rose sharply to Y128.15 = US$1 in 1988, though it fell slightly in the next two years to Y144.79 = US$1 in 1990 (Keizai Kôhô Centre 1995).

As the interest rate was progressively lowered in 1987, and easy money was available for speculation, the price of land and shares began to increase. Ever since the 1972–3 inflation occasioned by Tanaka Kakuei's plan for the 'redevelopment of the Japanese archipelago', land prices had been rising, imbuing people with the 'myth' that land prices would never fall. Also share prices were driven upwards by intensive corporate financial manoeuvring[1] helped by corporate cross-share holdings (Ogishima 1993). 'Easy money' encouraged the corporations to dabble heavily and aggressively in property speculation, by borrowing money which the banks as well as non-banks freely lent. Bank lending to the real-estate sector accounted for three-quarters of the Y81.5 trillion the real-estate sector required during the period 1985 to 1989, having grown 19.9 per cent on average annually, well above the annual 9.2 per cent average for all combined bank lending. The loans outstanding to the real-estate sector more than doubled in value, from about Y17 trillion to Y43 trillion. By 1989 the share of the loans to the real-estate sector accounted for 12.1 per cent of the total lending by the banking industry, a rise from 7.6 per cent in 1984. A further 18.8 per cent of the total outstanding bank loans went to the non-banks (Ministry of Finance Study Group 1993).

Japanese corporations also adopted aggressive programmes of *zaiteku*, namely financial engineering, aimed at boosting their income through investments in financial assets. Large corporations in particular, turned to the issue of commercial paper. They capitalized on the then high price of their stocks, and raised a huge amount of funds effectively at low cost through equity financing, well in excess of their capital shortfalls, thereby accommodating their growing reluctance to borrow from banks. In fact, such large companies as Toyota and Matsushita came to be known as the Toyota 'bank' and the Matsushita 'bank' because they not only had no borrowing from banks but they themselves had more than sufficient cash to meet their own capital needs. Large companies used their surpluses for amassing additional financial high-yield assets which became available since the financial deregulation of the mid-1980s. They, and even medium and small companies who were not in a position to procure funds through equity financing in the capital market, threw caution to the wind and went wild on a *zaiteku* spree.

It was not just the corporations which were caught up in the excitement of *zaiteku* in that period. Not only did the number of individual shareholders rise, from 16 million in 1985 to 24 million in 1989, but so did the volume of shares traded by them. These rose from an average of

58 billion shares per year during the first half of the 1980s to over 100 billion shares in the second half of the decade (Nihon Keizai Shinbun 1995). Behind the drive for investment in stock, was the sale of shares in the newly privatized Nippon Telegraph & Telephone Corporation (NTT) in 1986 and 1987, as well as NTT's subsequent listing on the stock exchange. Enormously oversubscribed, word of its share price movements, mostly upwards in the first years, was front-page news, and influenced the expectations of investors, many of whom had neither experienced nor expected losses through speculation. The Nikkei Stock Average went up from 12,755 in September 1985, clearing the psychological 20,000 in early 1987, to 38,915 at the end of 1989 thereby reaching its zenith. In parallel, the total market value of stocks in Japan rose from Y196 trillion to Y630 trillion at the end of 1989 (Ministry of Finance Study Group 1993). Corporate executives, bullish in their views on stock and in their outlook on the economy because of the higher real growth achieved in the GNP in the second half of the 1980s than was officially forecast, embarked upon an excessive level of capital investment. Firms also increased their recruitment of new school and college leavers towards the end of the decade, and there was a sudden and enormous scramble for first-time job seekers, particularly by the large companies, causing an acute labour shortage in the small and medium enterprise (SME) sector.

The rise of the yen against other currencies had its advantages, one of which was to boost Japan's economic standing in the eyes of the international community. Japan's per capita GNP stood at $11,000 as against $17,000 in the US in 1985. These figures changed to $19,500 for Japan and $18,500 for the US by 1987, with Japan topping all G7 countries (Keizai Kôhô Centre 1990). Similarly, Japan's financial industry was acquiring an increasingly prominent position in the world's financial market. Japanese banks and other financial-services institutions streamed abroad, enhancing the image of Japan as a big financial player. The Tokyo Stock Exchange came into prominence, joining the other two largest stock exchanges of New York and London thereby rendering trading in stocks a 24-hour global market, and displacing the US by 1989 as the country with the highest stock market capitalization in the world. Japan also displaced the US as the biggest creditor nation. Japanese money accounted for a large proportion of the US federal bond market (Harada 1994). In 1992, eight Japanese banks occupied the top eight positions in the world (according to *Fortune Magazine*, in JETRO 1994), and the four major securities companies have ranked among the world's top ten. The epithet 'financial superpower' came to be regularly used to emphasize Japan's economic strength.

The conspicuous spending by Japanese companies on properties and businesses which the high exchange rate of the yen facilitated, drew criticism from other nations. Acquisitions in real property, typified by Mitsubishi Real Property's purchase of the Rockefeller Centre in New York, and of other high-profile businesses, such as Sony's purchase of Columbia Pictures and Matsushita's acquisition of MCA, were but the tips of the iceberg. These high-profile acquisitions exposed Japanese business to critical reaction, particularly from the US.

As far as Europe was concerned, investment increased gradually from the beginning of the 1980s, essentially to avoid export embargoes and restrictions, but from about 1988 it began to gather momentum because of the advent of market integration in Europe in 1992. Though Japanese manufacturing investment accounted for about a quarter of the total inward investment in Europe, their presence drew attention because of their advanced and high-quality manufacturing technology, particularly in the automobile and electronics industry and further due to the Japanese management techniques which were adopted in their factories to support their operations. The total number of cases of manufacturing investment increased to over 700 by 1993 (JETRO 1994). Japanese manufacturing plants operating in the US and Europe presented highly visible cases of the transference of Japanese-style management, in terms of such practices as quality circles (QC), total quality control (TQC), zero defect (ZD), just-in-time (JIT), *kaizen*, as well as the single-status conditions and no or single union arrangements. In Europe, the UK was by far the most favoured country for locating manufacturing. The much publicized location of Nissan Motors' UK subsidiary in the North East in 1985 spawned the notion of the 'Japanization' of British industry in the late 1980s (Wicken 1987; Ackroyd *et al.* 1988; Oliver and Wilkinson 1990).

Throughout the 1980s the ratio of shares in corporate hands (all financial companies except investment trusts and securities companies, and business firms) increased, reaching over 70 per cent of the total shares issued by the late 1980s. The position which the financial companies occupied in shareholding is remarkably strong in Japan as is shown as Table 2.1. Altogether they owned over 46 per cent of the total shares issued in 1987. Of these, 16.4 per cent was held by the banks, 10.3 per cent by trust and banking, 13.1 per cent by life insurance companies, 4.1 per cent by general insurance and the remainder by others (Okumura 1991). The predominance of the banks in the equity market is a characteristic of Japan, certainly in strong contrast to the US as direct shareholding by commercial banks in the US is forbidden by law. For example, in 1987 Daiichi Kangyo Bank was the largest shareholder of 40 major companies, the second largest shareholder of 59 companies, and the third largest of 73 major companies. The figures for the Mitsubishi Bank are 36, 50 and 57 respectively, and those of Fuji are 33, 72 and 78, despite the limit of 5 per cent imposed on their holding of the shares of any single company since 1977. The banks also became the major shareholders to maintain and strengthen the lender position over the borrower companies, though the gearing ratio remained high (the equity capital ratio in 1977 was 14.1 per cent: Nakamura 1981). Banks held shares essentially for the exercise of control over the issuing companies and for group solidarity but not primarily for speculative purposes. Banks have remained closely integrated structurally with industrial capital in what one would call the *dirigiste* economy of Japan (Minami 1994). But in the late 1980s when corporations were able to raise large amounts of capital on the stock market to service their capital needs, as well as accumulate large reserves from profits, the influence of the banks was reduced.

THE 1990s

Introduction

The last decade of the twentieth century began for Japan with the destruction of the 'bubble', the result of which has caused a prolonged recession. This recession, however, has proved different from any other Japan has experienced since the war. This section attempts to describe the elements of the recession which are new to the experience of Japanese business, and how these new elements are affecting Japanese business organizations.

The state of the economy

At the hint of rising inflation, the government in July 1989 began to tighten the money supply by raising interest rates. Interest rates rose progressively to 6 per cent by July 1991. Not surprisingly, the 'bubble' began to deflate, and the stock market collapsed in early 1992. Property prices, which reached their peak in 1990 with a total value of Y2,389 trillion, began to fall from 1991 onwards. The fall in the growth rate from 4.3 per cent in 1991 to 1.1 per cent in 1992, was viewed as a normal cyclical reaction. When a historic cold and wet summer in 1993 resulted in a negative GDP growth of −0.2 per cent, and was followed by a growth which just cleared the zero point in 1994, it was realized that this recession was not only serious and the longest since the war, but a phenomenon fundamentally different to what had been previously experienced. The average corporate current profits fell by 18 per cent in 1994 from the previous year, clocking up the fourth consecutive year of industrial decline. Furthermore, industry was suffering from over-capacity, resulting from over-investment in the boom years. Certain household name companies had not just been suffering from a fall in current profit but had actually been failing to remain in profit at all.

What makes the current recession particularly serious is the existence of three new features, unfamiliar in recent Japanese business experience. The first is the continuous decline of land and stock prices undermining faith in them as sources of investment, and changing the basic assumptions driving investment and spending by business organizations. The second is the position of the Japanese banks. For the first time since the end of World War II, their relative immunity from the negative effects of business cycles has been challenged, due to an ever-increasing number of under-performing loans, causing a deterioration in the banks' financial position and in the quality of their lending. In fact, whilst aggregate net business profits of Japan's twenty-one major banks are estimated to have fallen by 6 per cent in the fiscal year 1993 from the previous year, their current profits position for the same year end has dropped by 40 per cent. The difference reflects net business profits used to write off bad debts (Ikeya 1994). However, this was not the end of their problems, as by the end of September 1994, the total value of bad debts disclosed by the twenty-one major commercial banks amounted to over Y13 trillion (Nihon Keizai Shinbun 27 March 1995). The banks have more problems to face since the properties they took as collateral have still fallen in value. So long as the banks remain saddled with these huge bad debts, the recovery of the stock market will not occur, nor will that of the economy.

Third, the yen has appreciated quite sharply since the beginning of 1993, breaking through the psychological Y100 = US$1 in June 1994, and continuing to rise to Y90 in March 1995 and up to Y83 to the dollar in early April. On 19 April, it momentarily rose further to record Y79.75 = US$1, dealing a heavy blow to Japanese exports in three ways. First, the sharp appreciation came at a time when export industries were over-extended through over-investment, and over-employment. Worse still, the yen appreciated not just against the dollar as it had done in the latter half of the 1980s, but also against European and Asian currencies, making the goods produced in those countries particularly competitive, and their imports undercut the prices of home products. Second, the yen's sharp appreciation came when domestic demand was shrinking so that there was no room left to domestically absorb this reduction in exports. Consequently, companies were forced to cut back production over-capacity, or move their production facilities to the expanding Asian countries where labour costs are much lower. Although overseas production accounts for only about 7 per cent of the total Japanese manufacturing output which is far lower than the 20 per cent level in the US, this proportion for the export-oriented industries has risen to 36 per cent (Nihon Keizai Shinbun 1995). Third, US manufacturers, particularly in automobiles and electronics where Japanese exports had been strong, have returned with strong competitive products (Nihon Keizai Shinbun 8 June 1994). The US government is pressing hard to remove the export barriers to Japan, which culminated in the US threat to invoke the 'Super 103' of the US Trading and Competitiveness Act of 1988 on all large Japanese cars imported to the US in 1995, allowing the US customs to impose a duty of 100 per cent. The disaster was only averted through last-ditch negotiations between the two countries, in which a compromise has been reached (Nihon Keizai Shinbun 29 June 1995). But this will not be the last of such episodes as, with the ending of the cold war, the US is likely to see Japan as its strongest opponent.

In order to prevent the value of the yen going up further, the Bank of Japan alone spent $10 billion buying up dollars to stop its further fall in March 1995, but without success. At the end of April the cumulative dollar reserve burgeoned to US$150 billion, a new high, $30 billion more than was the case in December 1994 (Nihon Keizai Shinbun 18 April 1995). What the Ministry of Finance and the Bank of Japan have done so far to stop its rise seems to be limited. Their slowness to act, and the ineffectiveness of their measures, and reluctance of the government to respond to the call for further deregulation, combined to drive up the value of the yen. The drastic 20 per cent rise of the yen in the first three months of 1995 seemed to reflect government ineffectuality.

Politics

The year 1993 was a significant one for Japanese politics. The '55-system' was destroyed by the result of the general election of June 1993 when the Liberal Democratic Party's hegemony came to an end after thirty-eight years. The new cabinet, headed by prime minister M. Hosokawa, the one-time governor of Kumamoto Prefecture and the leader of the New Frontier Party (Shinshin-tô), was a coalition of several parties, mostly formed out of the old LDP. His main political aim was the reform of Japan's political and electoral system, a topic which had been the centre of discussion for some time. The passage of the ensuing Reform Bill in January 1994 brought to a close the six-year debate, but it also tore apart the stitching that held the patchwork of different groups with the result that the Hosokawa government fell. After the stopgap, two-month Hata government, the situation was resolved by a new coalition government led by the prime minister, T. Murayama. Japanese politics has seen seven prime ministers in as many years since 1988, reflecting the level of turbulence and confusion that existed and continues to exist in the political world (Uchida 1995).

The direct cause of the LDP's fall from power was a series of scandals that involved the government, especially the Recruit scandal of 1988 and the Sagawa affair of 1992. However, behind all this lay a more fundamental reason. The '55 system' of government could not adjust properly to the rapidly changing international political climate of the late 1980s and early 1990s, which was brought about by the end of the US–Soviet cold war, and internal economic and social conditions.

In contrast, the new Murayama government is a coalition of Liberal Democratic Party (LDP), New Party Sakigake (Harbinger), one of the new splinter groups from the old LDP, and Social Democratic Party of Japan (SDPJ), with the last of these providing the prime minister (Uchida 1995). With the LDP and the New Frontier Party (Shinshin-tô), another of the splinter groups, being the two main parties of the lower house of the diet and SDPJ coming in third place, the Murayama government has to tread carefully to maintain the coalition. Even so, the ineffectiveness of the government to respond to the emergency situation occasioned by the great Hanshin earthquake in January 1995 has lost him and the coalition what little confidence the public had in the existing political parties. The loss of confidence was reflected in the local election in April 1995 when the crucial posts of the governors of Tokyo and Osaka fell to non-party candidates, both of whom were entertainers, leaving the party politicians far behind in second place.

The first of the political reform programmes, including the revision of regulations concerning political funding and the introduction of a new electoral system for the lower house, will lead to a weakening of the 'golden triangle', the close-knit relationships that have developed over a long period between the government, civil servants and business. The next general election fought on the newly drawn electoral map will be a first step to the sweeping structural reform Japan needs (Uchida 1995). But an early general election is now not likely. The pressure of public opinion demanding policy priority for immediate measures to revive the economy on the Hashimoto government over the dissolution of the Lower House is growing. The most urgent of the economic issues is that of Housing Finance Specialist Corporation (*Jūsen*) established to deal with the huge problem of bad debts which the new government inherited when Mr Murayama, the previous prime minister, suddenly decided to quit during the New Year's holiday in 1996. Unless this issue is quickly dealt with, the signs of economic recovery which began to show up in many of the economic indicators in the latter half of 1995 will wither away. The popularity rating of the Hashimoto government in the latest opinion poll fell from 54.3 per cent to 36.7 per cent, 23 per cent in the last two months because of the government's inability to deal with the problem (Nihon Keizei Shinbun 12 March 1996).

In the present prolonged recession and social uncertainty, strong political leadership appears to be what the country sorely requires to get the country out of its doldrums. At this crucial time, some fifty years after World War II, Japanese politics needs to seize the opportunity to carry out the much needed structural reforms in preparation for the twenty-first century. What remains to be seen is whether the political courage required for forceful structural reform of the Japanese economy and society, will be forthcoming.

1995

Since 1992, the government has injected an extra Y40 trillion into the economy, and the Bank of Japan has lowered the official lending rate from 6 per cent to the historic low of 1 per cent in April 1995. However, industry, unsure of the prospect of economic recovery, has been cautious in investing in plant and equipment, except in Asia. Similarly, the banks, still shackled by enormous bad debts totalling Y8.8 trillion for the eleven city banks alone at the end of March 1995 (Nihon Keizei Shinbun April 1995) have become over-sensitive about risks and are unwilling to lend. On top of that consumption, which makes up 60 per cent of the GNP in Japan, has not been brisk because consumers feel unsure about future prospects. As the high yen squeezed profit, the Nikkei 225 Stock Average is staying at the 16,000 level. The significance of this is that the fall in the share price to this level has meant that the hidden profit on which the strength and long-term orientation of the Japanese corporations so much depended, is alarmingly decreasing. Because of Japanese company practice of recording the value of shares held at their purchase price as the book value, when the price of shares they held rose as it did in the late 1980s, the actual current value of the shares increased enormously. This difference between the purchase value and the current value is called *fukumieki* (the hidden profit) and companies could increase the liquidity by selling the shares at the current price.

However, when the share prices fell in 1995 to the 1986 level, all the shares bought since 1986 actually could show as a loss, *fukumison*, the hidden loss. For example, according to Daiwa Economic Institute's estimate, at the end of March 1995 the value of the hidden profit on the shares held by the major life insurance companies was Y3.9 trillion, which was less than one-tenth of its value at its peak in March 1989 (Nihon Keizai Shinbun 24 March 1995). Similarly, Nomura Economic Institute's calculation shows that the value of the hidden profit on the shares held by the eleven city banks declined almost by half in the six months to March 1995 alone, undermining further their ability to write off bad debts (Nihon Keizai Shinbun 25 April 1995). Not surprisingly, many companies are selling large numbers of the shares they hold in order to balance their books and to obtain the liquidity required to allow them to reduce their workforce. The shares acquired through cross-holding arrangements particularly forged in the late 1980s, no longer gives a considerable number of companies any advantage. Hence such shares are being disposed of in order to avoid risk. According to Nissei Basic Institute, the proportion of shares held in cross-holding arrangements in 1993 was 44.9 per cent, 3.2 per cent down on 1986, and this is expected to have decreased in 1994 since the value of the shares sold by corporations in that year exceeded by Y2.2 trillion the value of shares they bought, the highest ever recorded (Nihon Keizai Shinbun 25 April 1995). Thus, the traditional practice of cross-shareholding by Japanese corporations is under scrutiny, though it is unlikely to come under an immediate threat of disintegration as, some argue, it is neither inefficient nor unfair and the present trend of share disposal by the banks and major companies is only a temporary phenomenon (Kon'ya 1995).

The case of Mitsubishi Corporation, the general trading company of the Mitsubishi group and one of the three leading companies of the Mitsubishi group (Igarashi 30 May 1995), is instructive. The book value of the stocks it holds amount to Y1 trillion, but in terms of current stock prices, this amounts to Y2 trillion. Since its total assets are valued at Y6.4 trillion the stocks account for a large proportion of its overall value (Nihon Keizai Shinbun 7 April 1995). These stocks at current low prices yield only 2 per cent profit. The company considers that this is no longer enough to justify the existing level of the traditional cross-shareholding arrangements. The organization is intending to gradually reduce the proportion of the stocks which belong to this arrangement. If it sells these stocks then it must expect other companies to sell the stocks they hold of the Mitsubishi Corporation. In September 1994, 70 per cent of total stocks issued by Mitsubishi Corporation were held by companies mainly in the Mitsubishi group. The corporation regards it as unavoidable that other companies will sell its stocks over the next few years, so that its stock held by the stable shareholders will drop to 50 per cent of the total. Who will purchase these 20 per cent shares is crucial to the corporation since it is now common knowledge that 60 per cent must be held by stable shareholders in order to get through the annual shareholders' meeting without undue upset (Nihon Keizai Shinbun 7 April 1995). Interestingly, the corporation wishes to see the shares go to non-Mitsubishi institutional investors, and in particular to overseas investors so that the present level of shareholding by them, 6.7 per cent, can be increased to 10 per cent or more (Nihon Keizai Shinbun 7 April 1995).

In order to realistically achieve such a change of shareholding, however, the corporation is required to alter its management aims so that an emphasis is placed on raising its return on equity (ROE), one of the main indicators of business performance in the West but one which has been neglected by Japanese companies. At the end of the fiscal year 1994, the average ROE for all the listed companies in Japan went down to 2.04 per cent compared with 15 per cent for the US corporate average (Nihon Keizai Shinbun 25 July 1995). The corporation aims to achieve 6 per cent ROE by the end of March 1998 and 8 per cent by 2001, and is reviewing the effectiveness of the management of its assets, including the stocks through cross-shareholding arrangements (Nihon Keizai Shinbun 7 April 1995). The importance of ROE as the indicator of performance is going to increase, as more stocks hitherto held through cross-shareholding arrangements come onto the market. Though many executives are still positive about cross-shareholding as a device necessary to allow them to pursue a long-term vision, the existing merits of such an arrangement are seen to weaken as time goes on (Okumura 1994b).

The high yen has also encouraged many businesses to switch their sourcing of parts from domestic companies to overseas firms in, for example, the newly industrializing economies (NIEs), the Association of the South East Asian Nations (ASEAN) and China, thus reducing the merit of holding shares of previous *keiretsu* suppliers. At the end of the fiscal year 1994, the proportion of shares held by the financial institutions (minus investment trusts) was down 3 per cent on 1989 to 39.3 per cent, by business firms down 1 per cent on 1989 to 23.8 per cent, and by private investors at 23.5 per cent, 0.9 per cent up on 1989. Further, the actual number of private investors decreased for the first time for twelve years, reflecting the decline in income, the worry about future employment prospects and the loss of confidence in the existing financial system. However, the proportion of shares held by foreign shareholders went up to 7.4 per cent, up by 3.9 per cent on 1989 and is the highest ever in post-war history and the fifth consecutive year to rise due to 'reacting to an expectation of the recovery of the Japanese economy by foreign investors' (Nihon Keizai Shinbun 1995). The low prices of 1994 made shares in Japan an extremely attractive source of investment. The 'mini-stock market' established by the Ministry of Finance and the Japan Securities Association jointly to encourage participation by more small, individual investors, began operating from July 1995 (Nihon Keizai Shinbun 19–20 April 1995). In this 'market' one can buy just one-tenth of the minimum number of shares one normally has to buy in a stock exchange, greatly reducing the amount of funding required to the average of Y75,000 (Nihon Keizai Shinbun 19 April 1995). Thus one should more easily afford to buy 100 shares of Toyota for around Y160,000 over the counter, instead of Y1.67 million for a bundle of 1,000, in which quantity, until recently, the majority of shares were sold in the Stock Exchange. The official lending rate set at 1 per cent is similar to the profit one can make on shares. With share prices at rock bottom, the new 'mini-stock market' might tempt first-time investors to switch from bank deposit to investing in stocks, leading to an increase in the proportion of individual shareholders (Nihon Keizai Shinbun 1995). The recession, worsened by the rapidly climbing yen and resulting in asset deflation, and a fall in asset prices in particular, is having far-reaching consequences on the capital structure of the economy. Another effect of the recession is on employment.

Manpower adjustment

One of the vital elements of successful Japanese management during the time of rapid growth was 'lifetime' employment (Okazaki-Ward 1993). Employers have, in the past, expected the cyclical trough to be followed by a rise in the economy, so they were reluctant to lose the expensively trained employees who would be difficult to replace when the economic upturn arrived (Keizai Dôyûkai 1994a; Kakabadse 1994). Apart from these reasons, employers are reluctant to be seen to break what amounts to a 'social contract' which is inherent in the notion of 'lifetime' employment and lose the commitment of the employees to the company (Harada 1994). In addition, there exists a concern today that, with the rapidly changing age profile of Japanese society, a new era of chronic labour shortage will dawn in the not too distant future, as Japanese society is ageing.

Yet, despite the concern over future labour shortages, this recession has resulted in an unemployment figure of over two million, that is a rate above the 3 per cent level, the worst in recent times. More than 90 per cent of listed companies are in the process of putting into effect certain employment reduction measures (Shigeta and Morita 1994) which is affecting white-collar employees, who have so far been mostly untouched by such an experience.

In the past, Japanese management has resorted to a range of measures to reduce the cost of labour when there was a recession, short of direct redundancy. However, the issue of low productivity of white-collar workers had not surfaced until the present recession, because past recessions were relatively short, and followed by a respectable growth rate (Sano 1993).

Also there have been changes in the nature of white-collar work through such developments as office automation and improved information technology, with the problem made more acute by the prolonged recession. One conservative estimate puts the 'in-company unemployed', kept on the company payroll by a combined funding from government grants and retained profits, at well over one million. These mostly consist of senior male white-collar workers belonging to what is known as the 'bulge' generation, the post-war baby boomers employed in the expanding late 1960s and early 1970s (*Tokyo Business Today* May 1993; Takanashi 1994). The 45-and-over age group is disproportionately large in the corporate age profile and forms the group with the highest labour cost. For example, in the late 1980s, if the salary of a 22-year-old graduate employed by a firm with 1,000 or more employees was taken as 100, that increased on average to 161 for those aged 30, to 254 for those aged 40, to 353 for those aged 50, and for those aged 55, it was 377, and thereupon fell to 348 for those aged 60 (Japan Productivity Centre 1989). In other words, an employee would double the salary he started with by the age of 35, treble by the age of 45, and by the age of 55 with a seniority of 33 years, an average of all industries was 3.46 times the initial salary. With the continued fall in profits and the prolongation of the recession, the head count reduction of this group has become inevitable. Initially, cases of permanent lay-off of some managers aged 50 years and above planned at TDK and the enforced early retirement of some managers above the age of 50 at Pioneer, were sensationalized by the media (*Tokyo Business Today* May 1993). However, a continuous stream of labour reduction plans by other companies has followed. The emphasis has now shifted to voluntary early retirement, which is made attractive by an offer of an enhanced retirement allowance, a measure fairly widespread by the end of 1994. IBM Japan began offering enhanced early retirement packages in 1992. NTT, the largest employer in Japan with 230,000 employees, has planned to reduce that number by 30,000 by 1996, 10,000 of these through voluntary retirement (Chûma 1994). In fact NTT achieved a reduction of 14,000 in the six-month period before March 1994, through a combination of early retirement, natural wastage and a reduction in the intake of new employees (Shigeta and Morita 1994). Shin-Nittetsu (Nippon Steel), the largest steel producer in the world with over 50,000 employees, is planning a reduction of 7,000 employees (4,000 of whom are white-collar) between 1994 and 1997 (Nihon Keizai Shinbun 1994). They actually managed, by March 1995, to have 5,000 employees accept severance through the offer of an enhanced severance allowance. The cost was offset by the sale of 60 million shares, mainly of Mitsubishi Bank and the Industrial Bank of Japan, held by the company (Nihon Keizai Shinbun 1995).

Though the need for reforming the practice of 'lifetime' employment is generally recognized, there still is a considerable reluctance to support its complete demise. The anxiety over lifetime employment is reflected in a large number of surveys carried out on this topic (Keizai Dôyûkai 1994c; Nihon Seisansei Honbu April 1994; Tokyo Chamber of Commerce and Industry April 1994; Seimei Hoken Bunka Sentaa 1994; Bank of Japan 1994; Nomura Research Institute 1994; Rômu Gyôsei Kenkyûsho 1994; all reported in Rôsei Jihô 8 April 1994). These surveys show a support for continuing the practice from just about half of the respondents, though in one study the rate was as high as 90 per cent. So long as the merits are considered by the employers to outweigh the disadvantages, the practice will be maintained. However, the scale of 'lifetime' employment is bound to change. The high proportion of the companies listed on the Japanese stock exchanges undertaking a reduction in the number of core employees (Nihon Nôritsu Kyôkai 1994; Shigeta and Morita 1994) has stimulated a debate amongst academics in Japan, some arguing that the 'lifetime' employment system is crumbling (Nihon Keizai Shinbunsha 1994), whilst others even advocate that it had never existed (Okuda 1994; Shimada 1994; Takanashi 1994). What occurred, the latter claim, has been a practice of long-term stable employment which emerged as a consequence of a sustained and rapid expansion of the economy, within which companies hungry for labour were too busy securing and retaining employees to even think of reducing them. De facto stable employment emerged fostering mutual expectations and trust between the employer and the employed. However, lifetime employment has not existed as a written legal contract.

Reflecting these recent changes, an attempt to review and to reformulate the future of the employment paradigm has been made by the Nikkeiren (Nihon Keieisha Danta Renmei 1995). In its report, compiled from the results of a survey carried out in the spring of 1994, it reiterates the centrality of the existing twin philosophy of 'long-term orientated management' and 'people-centred management', but acknowledges the continuity of the recent trend of increased inter-firm job mobility into the future. The Nikkeiren Report offers a new paradigm for future employment whereby the labour force reflects a mixture of long-term stable employees, mobile specialist employees, and fixed-status clerical employees (see Figure 2.1).

In keeping with such developments, remuneration is expected to shift towards a merit-based system. Even the increasingly popular system of annual salaries for white-collar employees rewarding ability rather than mere seniority, will become more the norm. If the practice of 'lifetime' employment is slow to diminish, the decline of the seniority system of promotion will be rapid. This will mean quite a radical shift in the management of personnel from unitary treatment to individualistic considerations in terms of rewards, promotion and development. It also means the development of evaluation systems which are seen to be fair and valid by the employees.

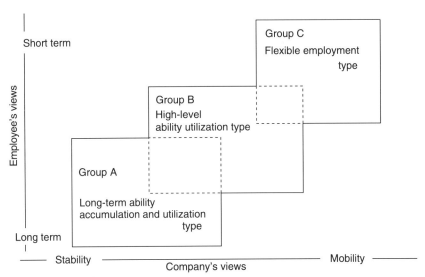

Figure 2.1 Relationships of company and employee in terms of employment and length of continuous service
Source: Nihon Keieisha Dantai Renmei, May 1995

Every indication is that there is no way back to wholly traditional employment practices. The steep rise in the yen in 1995 has caused further falls in profits, and even Toyota, which has been the most profitable company in Japan for the last several years, and has prided itself on being able to defend traditional employment systems, is finding itself unable to remain untouched by the high yen rate (Nihon Keizai Shinbun 4 and 5 May 1995). With the dollar exchange rate at Y84, the high yen will drive more Japanese companies to manufacture abroad. Clearly, human resources management is in a state of flux, and so long as the yen remains high and the share prices low, the speed at which change will occur is going to increase. Senior executives are equally not exempt from such pressure. Already a question is raised about the restructuring of corporate boards which are seen to be carrying too many 'time-server' directors (Kobayashi 10 October 1994; *Tokyo Business Today* 1994; Shigeta and Morita 1994).

Issues of corporate governance

In addition to these fundamental structural changes forced upon the Japanese economy and business organizations, top executives in Japan also face new and testing challenges. Harsh criticisms began to surface towards the end of the 1980s concerning various scandals, starting with, as stated, the Recruit Cosmos scandals in 1988 and extending to securities, finance, construction and distribution, and involving politicians, the civil servants and top management. Questions as to which institutional measures would be needed to check the actions of top management began to be voiced. What has forced the issues of corporate governance to come to the surface was the Japan–US Structural Impediment Initiative (SII) (1989–92) designed to examine the barriers that existed to affect trade between Japan and the US. One of the barriers identified by the US side was the closed nature of Japanese business through the 'inter-corporate network' web of relationships. Also pointed out was the near absence of shareholder influences as a checking mechanism on Japanese top management. The argument put forward was that Japanese corporations in relation to other foreign businesses were not playing on a level playing field. Such development has led to a dramatic rise in awareness of the issues of corporate governance in Japan in the 1990s (*Tokyo Business Today* May 1993).

What of the impact of shareholders on the issues of corporate governance? The unique features of the Japanese corporate world, namely the still high level of shares held by business organizations, the existence of *kigyô shûdan* (business groupings) held together by mutual and stable shareholdings amongst their members, supported by each grouping's presidents' club (see Table 2.2) which can be likened to an association of

Table 2.2 The six major business groupings (*kigyô shûdan*) in Japan

	Mitsubishi	Mitsui	Sumitomo	Fuyô	DKB	Sanwa

Name of the presidents' club	*Kinyôkai (Friday Club)*	*Nimokukai (Second Thursday Club)*	*Hakusui-kai (White Water Club)*	*Fuyô Club*	*Sankinkai (Third Friday Club)*	*Sansuikai (Third Wednesday Club)*
Financial services	Tôkyô Mitsubishi[a] Bank Mitsubishi Trust and Banking Meiji Mutual Life Tôkyô Marine and Fire	Sakura Bank Mitsui Trust and Banking Mitsui Mutual Life Taishô Marine and Fire	Sumitomo Bank Sumitomo Trust and Banking Sumitomo Life Sumitomo Marine and Fire	Fuji Bank Yasuda Trust and Banking Yasuda Mutual Life Yasuda Fire and Marine	Daiichi Kangyô Bank Asahi Mutual Life Taisei Fire and Marine Fukoku Mutual Life Nissan Fire and Marine Kankaku Securities Orient Lease	Sanwa Bank Tôyô Trust and Banking Nippon Life Orix

Table 2.2 continued

	Mitsubishi	Mitsui	Sumitomo	Fuyō	DKB	Sanwa
Name of the presidents' club	Kinyōkai (Friday Club)	Nimokukai (Second Thursday Club)	Hakusui-kai (White Water Club)	Fuyō Club	Sankinkai (Third Friday Club)	Sansuikai (Third Wednesday Club)
Trading and retailing, services, etc.	Mitsubishi Shōji Mitsubishi Research Institute	Mitsui Bussan Mitsukoshi	Sumitomo Shōji	Marubeni Shōji	C. Itoh Nisshō Iwai Kanematsu Kawashō Seibu Department Store Itōki Orient Corporation Tōkyō Dōmu	Nisshō Iwai Nichimen Iwatani International Takashimaya Orix
Cars	Mitsubishi Motors	Toyota Motors[b]		Nissan Motors	Isuzu Motors	Daihatsu Motors
Metals	Mitsubishi Steel Mfg. Mitsubishi Materials Mitsubishi Aluminium Mitsubishi Cable Industries Mitsubishi Copper	Japan Steel Works Mitsui Mining and Smelting	Sumitomo Metal Industries Sumitomo Metal Mining Sumitomo Electric Industries Sumitomo Light Metal Industries	NKK	Kawasaki Steel Kōbe Steel Japan Metals and Chemicals Nippon Light Metal Furukawa Electric Furukawa	Kōbe Steel Nakayama Steel Works Hitachi Metals Nisshin Steel Hitachi Cable

Mining and forestry		Mitsui Mining Hokkaidō Colliery and Steamship	Sumitomo Forestry Sumitomo Coal Mining			
Computers, electronics and electrical equipment	Mitsubishi Electric	Tōshiba	NEC	Oki Electric Industry Yokogawa Electric Hitachi	Fijitsū Fuji Electric Yasukawa Electric Mfg Nippon Columbia Hitachi	Iwatsu Electric Sharp Nittō Denkō Kyōcera Hitachi
Construction	Mitsubishi Construction	Mitsui Construction Sanki Engineering	Sumitomo Construction	Taisei	Shimizu	Tōyō Construction Obayashi Sekisui House Zenitaka
Chemicals	Mitsubishi Kasei Mitsubishi Gas Chemical Mitsubishi Plastics Industries Mitsubishi Resin Mitsubishi Kasei Polytec	Mitsui Tōatsu Chemicals Mitsui Petrochemical Industries	Sumitomo Chemical Sumitomo Bakelite	Shōwa Denkō Nippon Oil and Fats Kureha Chemical Industry	Kyōwa Hakkō Kōgyō Denki Kagaku Kōgyō Nippon Zeon Asahi Denka Kōgyō Sankyō Shiseidō Lion	Ube Industries Tokuyama Soda Hitachi Chemical Sekisui Chemical Kansai Paint Tanabe Seiyaku Fujisawa Pharmaceuticals

Table 2.2 continued

	Mitsubishi	Mitsui	Sumitomo	Fuyō	DKB	Sanwa
Name of the presidents' club	Kinyōkai (Friday Club)	Nimokukai (Second Thursday Club)	Hakusui-kai (White Water Club)	Fuyō Club	Sankinkai (Third Friday Club)	Sansuikai (Third Wednesday Club)
Industrial equipment	Mitsubishi Heavy Industries Mitsubishi Kakōki	Mitsui Engineering and Shipbuilding	Sumitomo Heavy Industries	Kubota Nippon Seikō	Niigata Engineering Iseki Ebara Kawasaki Heavy Industries Ishikawajima-Harima Heavy Industries	NTN Hitachi Zōsen Shin Meiwa Industry
Shipping and transportation	Nippon Yūsen Mitsubishi Warehouse and Transportation	Mitsui OSK Lines Mitsui Warehouse	Sumitomo Warehouse	Shōwa Line Keihin Electric Express Railway Tōbu Railway	Kawasaki Kisen Shibusawa Warehouse Nippon Express	Novix Line Hankyū Nippon Express
Cameras and optics	Nikon			Canon	Asahi Optical	Hōya
Cement		Onoda Cement	Sumitomo Cement	Nihon Cement	Chichibu Cement	Osaka Cement
Real estate	Mitsubishi Estate	Mitsui Real Estate Development	Sumitomo Realty and Development	Tōkyō Tatemono	Tōkyō Dōme	

Oil and coal	Mitsubishi Oil			Tônen	Shôwa Shell Sekiyu	Cosmo Oil
Fibres and textiles	Mitsubishi Rayon	Toray Industries		Nisshinbô Industries / Tôhô Rayon	Asahi Chemical Industry	Unichika / Teijin
Rubber and glass	Asahi Glass		Nippon Sheet Glass		Yokohama Rubber	Tôyô Tire and Rubber
Food and beverages	Kirin Brewery	Nippon Flour Mills		Nisshin Flour Milling / Sapporo Breweries / Nichirei		Itôham Foods / Suntory
Pulp and paper	Mitsubishi Paper Mills	Oji Paper		San'yô-Kokusaku Pulp	Honshô Paper	
Total	29	26	20	29	48	44

Source: Higashide K., *Ekonomisto* 1995: 55

Notes: Some companies belong to more than one business grouping.

[a] Tokyô Mitsubishi Bank, the result of a merger between Tokyo and Mitsubishi Banks, will operate officially from April 1996

[b] Toyota Motors is an observer

According to the result of an investigation by the Fair Trading Commission, the Presidents' Club usually meet once a month (except for the Daiichi Kangyo group which meets every three months) for the duration of between one and two hours. Not all members attend all meetings. The purpose of the meeting is to hear lectures on the current domestic and international affairs given by an outside speaker or club members, hear reports of donations and group events, but no discussion of individual companies' operational activities or attempt at co-ordinating the activities of the member companies takes place major corporate shareholders of each of the member companies, vertical corporate *keiretsu*, and the main bank system (Omura 1993; Fuji Sogo Kenkyusho 1993) have all protected Japanese corporate leaders from external scrutiny (Okumura 1991; Ito 1993; Nomura Sogo Kenkyusho 1992).

Because Japanese companies relied on debt financing for their long-term investment, interest rate burdens acted as a sort of restriction on investment decisions. Hence, the banks were deeply involved with management supporting corporate growth. Management, in turn, focused primarily on their main bank, their customers and on their own employees, aiming to expand their market share. Investors were satisfied, despite low dividends, so long as economic growth continued because of the capital gains that accrued to them. However, the switch to direct financing by corporations in the late 1980s and the share price plunge of the 1990s have changed the business environment. So far, the high level of corporate shareholding (around 70 per cent) and of cross-shareholding (45 per cent in 1988) allows major corporate shareholders to maintain the attitude of 'mutual non-interference' based on the tacit 'mutual acknowledgement of the trust' relationship (*sôgo shinnin*) (Okumura 1994b). In this way, top management is shielded from shareholder scrutiny. This is most prominently shown in the way the corporate annual general shareholders' meetings are held, even when many of the corporations have performed poorly as has been the case in recent years (Nihon Keizai Shinbun 30 June 1995). At the AGMs, the majority of which are held in June, approval of the report of the past year's operation and the contents of its proposals has largely become a ritual. The proceedings are uninterrupted because the large corporate shareholders usually submit no questions. Management's decisions rarely encounter a challenge from shareholders, *Sôkaiya* permitting.[2]

In general, the structure of the board of directors looks like the example shown below. The figures are taken in 1990 from a blue-chip company, and indicate the number of board members, with those in brackets being persons appointed from outside, two of whom were from the overseeing ministry and one from a public body who was the major customer. There were no non-executive directors (Okazaki-Ward 1993). The vast majority of Japanese boards do not have representatives of shareholder interests, are largely constituted by internal promotions, and are highly stratified in terms of status. The number of directors on boards varies, but most blue-chip companies will be found to have between thirty and forty directors. There are over 2,000 companies listed on the first section of the Japanese stock exchanges and of these the average number of directors per company in 1994 was 15.5 (Tôyô Keizai Shinpôsha 1994), though the number is much larger in the blue-chip companies which probably comprise about 10 per cent of the total listed on the first section of the stock exchange.

Board role titles: blue-chip company example

Chairman (*torishimariyaku kaichô*)	1	
President (*torishimariyaku shachô*)	1	
Vice-president (*torishimariyaku huku-shachô*)	3	(2)
Managing director (*senmu torishimariyaku*)	2	
Executive director (*jômu torishimariyaku*)	10	(1)
Director (*torishimariyaku*)	13	
Total	30	

Note: '*torishimariyaku*' means executive director as against non-executive director

The chairman of the board is usually the previous president and would have nominated the current president whose appointment would have been unanimously passed by the board. Once in office, the president practically wields absolute power over the appointment of his successor[3] and every other member of the board when their term of office comes up for renewal every two years, allowing him the opportunity to remove any director who is likely to oppose him or be controversial. After the appointment of the new president, drastic changes in the membership of the board are infrequent, though such changes do occur after an unexpected appointment (Keieijuku August 1995).[4] Dramatic changes are not looked upon favourably because of the cliques that may form around certain of the high-status directors, each one possibly promoting their view for change and which in turn is likely to lead to uncomfortable tension in relationships which may make the board a dysfunctional entity. The president, and one or more directors immediately below him in rank, and in some cases the chairman, are usually representative executive directors of the company (*daihyô torishimariyaku*), taking executive responsibility. The remainder of the board are expected to watch over their performance. Decisions are supposed to be taken by the board, but regularly the major strategic policy decisions are made by a small group of about half a dozen directors, with the president having the final authority. The remaining board members are usually reduced to endorsing the decisions already made.

Further, in accordance with commercial law, corporations must appoint internal auditors whose responsibility is to ensure financial propriety within the business. However, the practice up to now has been to have the internal auditors appointed by the president and most appointees are selected from an internal pool. Thus the president has substantial discretion in the choice of board directors and, understandably, it becomes difficult for board members to be openly critical of the top manager. Their continued tenure depends on their being compliant, knowing that their position on the board comes up regularly for renewal. Of course, new appointments have to be approved at the shareholders' AGM, where little or no opposition is usually encountered. By international comparison, company presidents are accorded an unusually powerful position in large Japanese organizations. The prevailing wisdom is that the exercise of such power is to attempt to ensure the health and the survival of the business.

However, changes occurring in the corporate environment are forcing the Japanese type of corporate governance to undergo revision. As already outlined, the 'bubble' loosened the influence of the main banks as companies could procure cheaper funding directly from capital markets. The resultant 'zaiteku' frenzy caused many executives to throw caution to the wind and speculate on a grand scale, only to find that they had been caught out when the stock market crashed. In addition, the high yen in the 1990s profoundly altered the situation. Hence, the debate over corporate governance is regarded by commentators and academics as timely, because they consider the present recession to be essentially the result of the absence of effective corporate governance in Japan (Tanaka August 1993).

Strong external pressures to make Japanese business more open has caused the Japanese government to bring in two revisions to the existing laws governing the conduct of directors. The first came into effect in October 1993 and required that an external auditor be appointed to the board in order to provide a more objective check on management accountability. However, the effectiveness of this measure is somewhat marred. A survey carried out by the Society of Auditors in Japan one year later reveals that 42.2 per cent of external auditors have been internal appointments or were members of the parent companies, hence lacking independence and objectivity (Shigeta and Morita 1994). The same authors also refer to the ineffectiveness of directors appointed from outside to check the performance of the remaining members of the board.

The second reform involves the cost of litigation for damages caused to the company by the actions of management which are considered as illegal or negligent of their statutory duties. The cost of court action by a representative shareholder has been brought down from Y235 million to a mere Y8,200 (Tanaka August 1993). Already by the middle of 1994, thirteen cases involving nine companies and over 200 torishimariyaku and auditors had been brought to court, with the total compensation being demanded amounting to Y337 billion (Nikkei Business May 1994). A simple calculation shows that, on average, each executive involved is being sued for over Y1.5 billion in damages, a sum well beyond their personal financial capability. Becoming a torishimariyaku, once regarded as the ultimate goal for corporate employees, is not going to remain the unclouded pinnacle of achievement it once was. Today any shareholder who has held shares in a company for six months qualifies to sue members of that company's board for damages on behalf of the company (Nikkei Business 9 May 1994). With this reform, shareholders will press for disclosure of more detailed financial information from the company. An increase of foreign investors and institutional shareholders will mean that Japanese companies will be forced to adopt international standards of accounting practices (Tanaka May 1993), and to take account of shareholders' interests on the board. The recent entry of CALPERS (California Public Employee Retirement System) of the US into the Japanese equities markets, the organization known to have been behind the recent spate of changes at the top of major US firms such as GM, IBM, Westinghouse and American Express, is likely to add pressure on Japanese executives to pay more heed to the interests of the shareholders, and to redress the balance, so far too heavily tipped against shareholder interests (Nikkei Business May 1994).

Another reform concerning company liability for its products is equally promoting change in the arena of corporate governance. The product liability laws came into force in July 1995. With only six short clauses, this piece of legislation has been causing considerable apprehension in industry. Basically, it makes the producer liable for compensation for damages and injury clearly caused by a defect in a product sold, even if the defect in the product was not the producer's fault. The law also shortens the time of litigation and reduces legal costs. The consumer no longer has to prove that damage, or injury was caused by fault(s) in the product, as has been the case until now. An indication of how cumbersome and unhelpful the old law was to the consumer is shown in the fact that between 1945 and 1995, only around 200 cases had been brought to court (Hayashida 30 June 1995). Manufacturers from now will have to be much more sensitive and mindful towards consumer safety and satisfaction. The need to be prepared to manage risks positively (Kagono 30 June 1995) and to become more aware of the legislation concerning consumer rights, will be of paramount concern for the future.

Another aspect of customer orientation is brought to notice by the recent revolt of some retail heavyweights against the dictates of the manufacturers in terms of pricing. These retailers are leading a phenomenon called 'price destruction', namely an attempt to make products available at much more reasonable prices to customers, who in turn are now keenly conscious of the large 'price gap' between the yen's purchasing power abroad and in Japan. This is one reason why people feel that they are not getting a fair share of the country's economic success (Keieijuku June 1994).

These recent changes of legislation do expose corporate executives to higher risks, and force them to take more serious cognizance of the wider community of stakeholders, apart from the employees and banks, such as institutional and individual shareholders, customers, consumers in general, local communities and environmental and political pressure groups. The challenge they face under the current deflationary economic condition is immense. With so many fundamental changes occurring, it is not surprising that in the 1990s, just when Japan has reached the position of global eminence achieving the national goal set some 130 years ago, it is now facing a new challenge described as the third turning point in the modern history of Japan (Keizai Dôyûkai 1994a).

Clearly, many corporations are facing an extremely difficult time, and their future is not clear to see. The question is what capabilities do Japanese business leaders need to have to respond to such challenges and lead the businesses through the turbulent and uncharted global economic seas of the 1990s and beyond? Will they require a different calibre of leadership than hitherto? Will Japanese business organizations need a different kind of development from the largely in-company-based system and also is such an alternative available? Will a reform of boardroom structure be required?

The international study and the recommendations for executive development outlined in the next chapters go some way to addressing these concerns. The age, background, job and organizational profile of top Japanese managers are presented. Further, specific attention is given to issues of management philosophy and style. It is highlighted that a new breed of Japanese managers is emerging, confronting problems such as rising costs and through their actions emphasizing the need for Japanese business organizations to adopt approaches more suited for a difficult and stormy future. Integrating such a variety of approaches becomes a crucial management development challenge which is addressed in the final chapter on both a national and international basis.

NOTES

1 According to Okumura, the *antei kabunushi kôsaku* allows an issuing corporation's floating shares to be bought up purposely by other corporations who are stable shareholders of its shares, thereby raising the price of its shares on the market. He argues that, basically, the *antei kabunushi kôsaku* is carried out jointly by the issuing company and a securities firm, which can lead to a control on the supply–demand relationship of the shares on the market by the securities firm. The ability of the securities companies to control the markets has been used for speculative purposes, pushing up the share prices (Okumura 1994).

2 For the fiscal year 1994, 2,110 AGMs were held on 29 June by the companies

who had closed their accounts at the end of March, according to the National Police Agency (Nihon Keizai Shinbun 30 June 1995). This was by far the largest number of shareholder AGMs held on a single day so far. Until recently companies had been apprehensive of AGMs because of the possible, and staged, disturbances and interruptions. These disruptions were caused by a group of people called *Sôkaiya* (AGM specialists) who attended as shareholders with the clear intention of upsetting the meeting, sometimes including violence to intimidate the management.

The origin of *Sôkaiya* goes back to pre-war times and was set in the background of the gangland. They were used by big businesses to settle their internal disputes behind the scenes (Okumura and Sataka 1992). Since the war their connections with many big businesses have been maintained, but their silence at the AGM has been bought expensively. They continued to find and extort money from new corporate victims. This situation eventually led to a revision in commercial law in 1981 which made illegal all such payments. One of the consequences of this restriction has been an increase in violent disturbances at AGMs.

Regarding the 2,110 AGMs held in 1995, both the sheer number of companies holding meetings on the same day and the police involvement signify the organized strategies of the businesses to deal with these threats. As a measure of their success, the great majority of the AGMs were over peacefully in around thirty minutes. However, it was reported that many lacked a sense of urgency on the side of management despite the fall in the value of their shares and poor performance. Commenting on this, William Christo, President of CALPERS, is reported to have said that it reflected the general attitude of Japanese business, i.e., taking little notice of the opinion of its shareholders (Nihon Keizai Shinbun 30 June 1995).

3 The appointment of Mr N. Idei to the presidency of SONY created quite a sensation, all the more so because it was a very closely kept secret which took even directors of SONY by surprise when it was announced at the special board meeting at the end of March 1995. 'By surprise', because Idei, the youngest *jômu torishimariyaku*, was chosen over thirteen other directors senior to him, and he is the one without a technological background. Most directors had expected one of the vice-presidents responsible for technology to be chosen (Keieijuku May 1995: 34–48).

4 What happened in 1995 at Dentsû, an advertising giant with the largest accounts on their books in the world, is a case in point. The president, Mr T. Narita, who had been at his post since 1993, removed twelve directors from the top of the board, promoting his own followers to replace them. One of the retiring directors was the vice-president and Narita's rival for the post of president. Others were those who had been seen to be either in the rival camp or too neutral. Newly appointed *torishimariyaku* who filled the gap at the bottom of the hierarchy are also Narita's own men. His move can be seen to reflect his determination to have a 'team' at the top on whose total commitment he can depend, in order to push through the previous year's organizational restructuring, and to weather the current 'lean' period successfully (Keieijuku August 1995: 138–41).

Part II
The study

Chapter 3

The makings of a top manager

The most important criterion of leadership is how easily, or how willingly, you would transfer your knowledge to your subordinates. In other words, even if you are not there in person at any time, your subordinates can cover for you with confidence. That is an important assessment of leadership.

(Y. Fujisawa, Director, Toray Textile Europe Limited)

KEY ISSUES

Particular attention is given to understanding the leadership capabilities of top Japanese managers. Initially, a demographic analysis of role seniority, age, areas of responsibility, educational background, years in present job and years in present organization, is provided. Examination of the quality of dialogue that takes place between senior managers at the top of Japanese orgnanizations is equally undertaken, as are the behaviours of top Japanese managers. It is highlighted that quality of dialogue is poor, possibly because of the emergence of a new breed of manager who is focused, businesslike, attentive to detail and if necessary willing to sacrifice the existing culture of support for the achievement of results. Such emerging tensions in Japanese organizations are shown to have repercussions when managing on an international basis.

Are leaders born or made?[1] In order to study the successful men and women of the business world, should one examine what happens to people once in the top job or should one look at the attitudes and behaviours of senior people in order to understand the complexities of success? In this analysis of top Japanese managers, both the characteristics of the job and person undergo scrutiny. The manager's job is distinguished between the leadership elements and the managerial/administrative elements. It is assumed that the more senior the manager, the greater the emphasis that will need to be placed on the leadership side of the role. Such thinking makes sense, for each senior manager will need to make choices between unclear alternatives, is likely to need to devote considerable attention to nurturing key interfaces with influential key internal and external stakeholders, in order to ascertain their commitment to a meaningful way forward.

What choices are made and how commitment is negotiated, highlights the influence the stakeholders are likely to have on the organization, as well as the capabilities of senior managers to respond effectively to such challenges. There is no reason to assume that even if the capacity of top management in the organization is considerable, each of the members of the senior executive would form similar conclusions as to the shape, size, direction, desired qualities of the total organization and thereby the shape and cost of each of the key functions/divisions/business units in the organization. Hence, senior managers, sharing the same challenges to address, may form different views as to the configuration of their organization and how it should be led. Exploring each senior manager's beliefs concerning what to lead, how to lead and when to lead, highlights one key issue: to what extent do senior managers share their views and concerns with each other?

On this basis, fundamental to effectively leading an organization is to ensure a high-quality dialogue amongst the members of the senior executive. The preliminary results of interviews and case study analyses, examining the behaviours and capacities of senior managers, both in Japan and Europe, indicate that where the quality of dialogue is high and the relationships amongst senior managers is positive, the issues and concerns facing the organization are likely to be more openly addressed. Where, however, relationships are tense and the quality of dialogue restricted, certain issues and problems tend not to be raised, because to do so would generate unacceptable levels of discomfort amongst certain or all of the members of the senior executive. In effect, such discomfort would be experienced as too unwelcome in facing up to the problems confronting the organization. Ironically, the case studies highlight that unless the top team is working reasonably effectively, issues which need to be addressed are not: the senior management knowingly allows the organization to deteriorate because they feel too uncomfortable to jointly discuss and attend to key issues and challenges facing the enterprise.

Study design

We examined the relationship between individual attributes, roles and organizational requirements and quality of dialogue among senior Japanese managers. Comparison is made between the Japanese respondents and the respondents emanating from surveys conducted in eight European countries, namely, Britain, France, Germany, Sweden, Spain, Ireland, Austria and Finland through the Cranfield Executive Competencies questionnaire. Preliminary interviews and case study analyses conducted in Britain, Ireland, France, Sweden, Greece, Austria, Germany, Spain and in Japanese firms located in the UK, significantly influenced the design and content of the Cranfield Executive Competencies questionnaire. The questionnaire attempts to capture elements of national and organizational culture, as well as key attitudes and behaviours displayed by the managers observed in the initial case analyses. The structure of the questionnaire allows for comparisons to be made between different groups of respondents. Back translations and further screening were employed to ensure consistency in interpretation when translated from English into other languages.

Through the support and co-operation given by our partner, the Japan Management Association (JMA), questionnaires were distributed and collected in Japan. On the suggestion from colleagues at the JMA, the questionnaires were sent to named executives representing their companies who were asked to distribute the documents among their peers, and were returned by the respondents anonymously and direct to JMA to ensure freedom of expression. Altogether, 761 top Japanese managers completed the questionnaire. Over 2,500 top European managers also returned completed questionnaires.

Four key areas of exploration concerning Japanese senior managers are reported, covering:

- *issues of demography*, namely, age of incumbents, levels of educational background, areas of responsibility, numbers of years in present job and organization, and seniority of role;
- *the quality of dialogue* among the members of the senior executive, namely, the extent to which sensitivities within the senior group inhibit discussing key business concerns affecting the current performance and future of the organization. Further examination concentrates on how quality of dialogue in turn is likely to impact on the extent to which the members of the senior executive hold a shared view as to both the future direction of the organization and the issues to address to promote its well-being. Sensitivities refer to those issues and/or tensions in relationships which are perceived by the group members to be difficult to discuss, bearing in mind the different views and positions adopted by individual members, which impact on their relationship and in turn may negatively influence their openness of conversation;
- *the styles of leadership* adopted by different levels of Japanese manager, exploring whether the demands of different roles influence the attitudes and behaviours of managers and which, in turn, impact on the performance of the organization;
- *measures of organizational performance* are discussed in this paper as: *the opportunity costs* that are likely to arise if the members of the senior

executive exhibit poor quality dialogue and a lack of shared vision concerning the future and/or the manner in which the organization is to be enhanced; *sector differences* in terms of demographics, managerial values, manager behaviours and attitudes across the three sectors of manufacturing, retail and services are highlighted; *national differences* in terms of demographics, managerial values, manager behaviours and attitudes and styles across the eight European countries and Japan in each of the three sectors of manufacturing, retail and services which are examined with a view to identifying particular elements in each sector which may require attention in terms of management development.

Throughout, comparisons are made between the Japanese and other European respondents. Cluster (a mechanism for grouping respondents), regression (a statistical technique used for prediction) and correlation (a statistical technique measuring association) analyses are utilized to explore the relationship between certain of these characteristics. Finally, recommendations are made concerning how to meet the development needs of senior and high-potential Japanese managers.

ANALYSIS OF JAPANESE MANAGERS

Demographics

Information contained here emphasizes role seniority, age, areas of responsibility, educational background, years in present job, and years in present organization, giving the demographic characteristics of the Japanese top management in the study. Data on role seniority shows that the structure of the Japanese corporate board is tall, made up of six tiers. Given that seniority counts in the role positions, the over-representation of the presidents in the sample pervades other demographic data. Thus, 64 per cent of the sample are aged 56 or over, and 41 per cent of the respondents are responsible for the total company, and more than half of the total respondents have been with the company for more than twenty-one years. However, 70 per cent of the respondents have been in their present job for four years or less, reflecting the system of role allocation in the corporate board where directors are moved upwards or outwards regularly through the corporate hierarchy. Data on educational backgrounds is the only demographic characteristic where we attempted a comparison with the Cranfield European study results, even though the straight comparison was difficult because of the difference in education systems. The proportion of the Japanese sample who have post-A-level educational qualifications is much higher than those in the UK, Germany and France, but those with postgraduate qualifications is much lower than in those countries.

Role seniority

The respondents are classed as representing ten levels of organization.

Role seniority	No.	%
1 Owner of the business, chairman, vice-chairman	27	4
2 CEO, president	160	21
3 Vice-president	30	4
4 Senior managing director	78	10
5 Executive director	168	22
6 Director of the board	229	30
7 Auditor	12	2
8 Senior adviser	4	0.5
9 Non-board director	5	0.7
10 General manager, divisional manager	33	4
No response	15	2

Positions 1 to 6 comprise members of the board and account for 91 per cent of the total. Chairman/president group account for 25 per cent, vice-president/senior managing director group 14 per cent, and executive director/director 52 per cent. Of positions 1 to 4, numbering about six or fewer people, these typically comprise the members of the *jômukai* (executive board). The senior adviser is an ex-member of the board, and often ex-chairman. Non-board directors and general managers are the senior middle management of the organization, but the former usually do not have line management responsibility.

Age

Age	No.	%
Up to 40	7	1
41–45	29	4
46–50	53	7
51–55	187	25
56–60	294	39
61–65	149	20
65 and over	39	5
No response	3	0.4

Of the total, almost 88 per cent are aged 51 or above, and 25 per cent are aged 61 or over. Only 12 per cent are aged 50 or below.

Areas of responsibility

Areas of responsibility	No.	%
Total company	312	41
Number of divisions/departments	211	28
Single major division/department	175	23
Other combinations	50	7
No response	9	1

Forty-one per cent of the respondents, accountable for the total company, match closely the proportion of the sample population who occupy levels 1 to 4. These are usually the members of the executive committee, and are held accountable for the affairs of the total company. Executive directors are usually responsible for two or more departments, whilst the responsibility for a major division/department usually falls on the director.

Educational background

Educational background	No.	%
O-level equivalent	4	0.5
A-level equivalent	62	8
HND equivalent	26	3
BA, BSc	599	79
MA, MSc	38	5
MBA	8	1
PhD	23	3
Professional qualification	135	10
No public qualification	476	63

Of the total sample of senior managers, 9 per cent have qualifications up to only secondary-level education. Those who have undertaken undergraduate and HND equivalent programmes account for 82 per cent of the total, and a further 9 per cent have postgraduate degrees. Also 10 per cent have recognized professional qualifications.

A comparison of educational attainment with managers in the European study has proved to be difficult because of the different systems prevailing in each of the countries, and the only reliable way is to compare those with qualifications beyond A-level or its equivalent. On this basis, the Japanese respondents with post-A-level qualifications account for 91 per cent, whilst the figures for the UK, Germany and France are 59 per cent, 64 per cent and 86 per cent respectively. However, at postgraduate level, the figures reveal quite a different story, as 9 per cent of Japanese, 22 per cent of UK, 26 per cent of German and 42 per cent of French respondents hold postgraduate qualifications.

Years in job

Number of years in job		
	No.	%
<6 months	35	5
6–11 months	112	15
1–2 years	179	24
3–4 years	199	26
5–6 years	86	11
7–8 years	52	7
9–10 years	13	2
>10 years	77	10
No response	8	1

Two-thirds of the sample (69 per cent) have been in their current post for four years or less, with those who have been in the post for three to four years accounting for the largest number.

Years in company

As it usually takes twenty-eight years or more for one to become a board director in most large companies where 'lifetime' employment is the norm, the fact that nearly half of the respondents have been in their companies for more than twenty-six years is not surprising (Okazaki-Ward 1993). However, it is striking to find that 25 per cent of the respondents have been with the company for six years or less, particularly given that 88 per cent of the sample are aged 51 or over. (See section on 'Styles of leadership', particularly that on the business drivers.) One

Number of years in the company		
	No.	%
<6 months	3	0.4
7–11 months	22	3
1–2 years	35	5
3–4 years	72	10
5–6 years	53	7
7–8 years	36	5
9–10 years	26	3
11–15 years	43	6
16–20 years	45	6
21–25 years	67	9
26 years or more	365	47
No response	3	0.4

explanation could be that many of these respondents have recently been transferred to their current company from the parent company, or appointed from outside the company, for example from the government ministry, the main bank or other companies in the same *keiretsu* (group).

Quality of dialogue

Comparison is drawn between the Japanese and the European respondents. Exploration is undertaken in terms of differences of view that may exist concerning the future direction of the organization, those sensitive issues (if any) that the respondents consider merit, but do not receive, attention at top management levels and differences of view that may exist between top managers and their general managers at lower levels concerning key aspects of managerial behaviour.

Future direction

In terms of strategic intent, one key question is asked, namely, 'Do the members of the senior executive (i.e. presidents/CEOs/MDs/EDs/ GMs)[2] hold different views as to the future direction of the company?' (Table 3.1). Of the Japanese respondents, 23 per cent indicate that differences of view exist at senior management levels, concerning the shape of the organization and the future paths it should follow. The Irish highlight greatest differences of view, with 48 per cent of their respondents indicating diversity of perception at senior management levels concerning the direction the organization should pursue. The Swedish

Table 3.1 Fundamentally different views concerning the direction of the company (per cent)

	Japan	UK	France	Ireland	Germany	Sweden	Spain	Austria	Finland
Yes	23	30	39	48	32	20	40	31	25

Table 3.2 Sensitivities that merit attention but do not receive attention in top team (per cent)

	Japan	UK	France	Ireland	Germany	Sweden	Spain	Austria	Finland
Yes	77	47	36	68	61	50	63	67	49

respondents highlight the least degree of differences of view on strategic direction at senior management levels.[3]

Addressing sensitivities

In terms of issues requiring resolution at senior management levels, one question is asked, namely, 'Are there issues or sensitivities that merit attention but do not receive attention in the top team?' (Table 3.2). The Japanese respondents highlight the greatest number of concerns, with 77 per cent of the sample stating that important but unaddressed issues predominate senior management attention. The Irish sample highlights the second highest score with 68 per cent, closely followed by the Austrians and Spanish. The British, Finnish and French identify the least number of sensitive issues remaining unaddressed at senior management levels.

However, even with the French, for whom 36 per cent of their respondents identify outstanding issues remaining unaddressed at senior levels in the organization, the results highlight the strain senior managers are likely to experience in responding positively to difficult challenges. Hence, the nature and quality of the behaviour senior managers adopt in order to implement their intentions and decisions is considered to require examination.

Managerial behaviour

Six aspects of senior manager behaviour are explored, namely, approachability, addressing sensitivities, being understanding, being perceived as trustworthy, displaying commitment to decision implementation and being seen to address long-term and short-term issues (Table 3.3). Distinction is made between the responses of presidents, chairmen, CEOs, MDs, EDs, and those holding general manager (GM) and director positions. The aim is to identify whether compatibility of view exists between top-level managers and the general managers below them concerning the behaviour and effectiveness of the top team.

Overall, the Japanese respondents provide the greatest degree of compatibility of view. Similar responses across all of the country respondents emerge to the question, 'Are the members of the top team easy to talk to?' Only the Irish and German GMs consider their senior managers less approachable than their senior managers would consider themselves. In contrast, substantial differences of response across all the country respondents emerge to the question 'Do the members of the top team openly discuss sensitive issues?' Of Japanese top managers, 69 per cent consider they openly address sensitive issues, whereas 47 per cent of the Japanese GMs consider that the top team address safer issues.

Table 3.3 Managerial behaviours: comparative response by seniority (per cent)

	Japan		UK		France		Ireland		Germany		Sweden		Spain		Austria	
	Top	GM	Top	GM	Top	GM	Top	GM	Top	GM	Top	GM	Top	GM	Top	GM
Easy to talk to	82		73		80		87		78		84		75		80	
Not easy to talk to		62		65		76		41		54		83		77		64
Discuss sensitive issues	69		66		71		52		68		66		44		60	
Address safe issues		47		44		47		60		63		42		61		51
Understanding	78		68		61		52		41		63		53		58	
Not understanding		61		70		48		67		68		48		61		51
Trust each other	73		65		66		61		75		71		58		63	
Not trust each other		61		68		48		67		69		66		51		57
Implement decisions made in top team	89		72		74		91		83		79		70		65	
Implement decisions that personally suit		76		44		64		50		64		73		69		41
Address long- and short-term issues	75		54		58		61		68		56		61		62	
Address short-term issues		62		58		48		66		42		50		60		49

Note: Top: presidents/CEOscChairmen/MDs. GM: general managers

The Irish and Spanish responses err more on the negative side, whereby 52 per cent and 44 per cent respectively of top managers consider they more openly address sensitivities, whereas 60 per cent and 61 per cent of their GMs respectively consider that safe issues are discussed. In contrast, and more on the positive side, 68 per cent of top German senior managers consider they openly discuss sensitive issues and 63 per cent of their GMs agree.

Regarding the issue of being seen as understanding, Japan is the only country where the views of both the top managers and GMs are positive and supportive. In contrast, the percentage of GMs in the UK, Ireland, Germany and Spain who consider that their top managers do not understand each other is higher than the top managers themselves, who consider that they have a good understanding of each other. In France, Sweden and Austria, the percentage of top managers who consider that they understand each other is higher than that of their GMs who think that their top managers lack an understanding of each other.

On the issue of trust, the Japanese responses highlight similar levels of compatibility to the Swedes. For both samples, the top managers indicate that the levels of trust amongst the members of the top team is high, an opinion that is shared by their GMs. The greatest level of incompatibility of response arises from the Irish, UK and German respondents, whereby 67 per cent, 68 per cent and 69 per cent respectively of their GMs consider that the behaviour of top management is indicative of low levels of trust amongst the members of the senior executive.

Equally, compatibility of scores from the Japanese respondents emerge in response to the question, 'Do the members of the top team implement decisions jointly made in the top team?' Of the top management group, 89 per cent indicate they do and 76 per cent of their GMs agree. A contrast of scores between the top management group and the GM sample is identified by the British, Irish and Austrian respondents. The Irish respondents provide for the greatest contrast, with 91 per cent of top management indicating that decisions jointly made in the top team are implemented, whereas 50 per cent of their GMs consider that their senior managers implement only those decisions that personally suit the individual, irrespective of whatever was jointly agreed.

In response to the question, 'Do the members of the top team address long- and short-term issues?', the Japanese respondents provide the most comparable, positively oriented responses. Of the respondents in the top management category, 75 per cent consider that they address both long- and short-term issues and 62 per cent of the Japanese GM sample agree. The Spanish respondents highlight compatible but negatively oriented responses whereby 61 per cent of top management and 60 per cent of the GMs consider that the top team address only short-term issues. For the remaining respondents, differences of view are identified between senior managers and the GM group.

STYLES OF LEADERSHIP

Through cluster analysis (Everitt 1981), utilizing role seniority, length of time in present job, length of time in present organization and age of respondents – three distinctly different groups of respondents emerge from the Japanese sample. The reason for undertaking a cluster analysis of the above demographic items is to explore their impact on the attitudes, values and behaviours of Japanese managers, bearing in mind that writers such as Wiersema and Bantel (1992) suggest managers' flexibility decreases and rigidity and resistance increase, as people age.

Subsequently, factor analysis of attitudinal and behavioural questions was undertaken within each of the clusters, emerging with distinctly different combinations of attitude and behavioural characteristics between the three groupings (Rummel 1970). Interestingly, age of respondents is identified as having no significant impact on the clusterings. Therefore, it is concluded that the significant determinants of senior managers' attitudes towards jobs, people in the organization and the organization itself, are seniority of role, length of time in current job and length of time in organization.

Three groups of leaders emerge from the analysis of Japanese organizations. The first group are those managers holding senior office, whose fundamental pre-occupation is the discussion of and generation of policy (policy makers). The second group are those managers whose primary concern is the achievement of objectives and the meeting of targets for the company (business drivers). The third group are those managers whose primary concern is with the implementation of strategy (implementors).

Japanese leadership characteristics

Table 3.4 identifies the key demographic characteristics of the three management styles in terms of role seniority, length of time in the organization and also in the job.

Profile of the policy makers

The policy makers are more likely to be currently holding a senior role such as chairman or chief executive officer (CEO), vice-president (VP) or senior managing director (SMD) role and have been in the company and held their position for a substantial period of time. In terms of size of the company, policy makers are scattered – 47 per cent work in small to medium-sized organizations (up to 500 employees), 27 per cent in

Table 3.4 Demographics of leadership

Manager style	Role seniority	Years in company	Years in job
Policy makers (*n* = 204)	Chairmen President/CEO VP/SMD	Over 20 years	Over 10 years
Business drivers (*n* = 213)	SMD Executive director Director	Under 5 years	3 years average
Implementors (*n* = 285)	Director GM	Over 20 years	Under 2 years

Note: Total = 702. The remaining 59 respondents were not classified due to missing data.

medium-sized organizations (500 to 2,499 employees) and the remaining 26 per cent work in large organizations (2,500 or more employees). Policy makers are identified as mainly in manufacturing (57 per cent), the remainder being split into retail (14 per cent) and services (29 per cent).

Profile of the business drivers

The business drivers are people who are more likely to hold senior managing director (SMD), executive director or director roles, and have been in the same job for about three years on average and are likely to have been employed in the same company for a limited period, namely under five years. Some have been employed for up to ten years, but none longer than that.

By way of company size, like the policy makers, business drivers are scattered but more towards organizations with 2,499 or fewer employees: 48 per cent work in small to medium-sized organizations (up to 500 employees), 36 per cent in medium-sized organizations (500–2,499 employees) and the remaining 16 per cent work in large organizations (2,500 or more employees). This grouping differs from the other two groups in terms of industry sector, there being roughly an even split between those from manufacturing (44 per cent) and those from services (46 per cent). The services sector is considered as volatile, which could explain why some have been in the company for a limited period of time. Further, those from the manufacturing sector may have been transferred to their current company from their parent company. The remaining 10 per cent in this category are from the retail sector.

Profile of the implementors

The implementors may occupy a directorship but are more likely to hold a GM position, are more likely to have been in their present job for under two years (certainly no longer than four years) but have been employed by the company for a substantial period of time. In effect, the implementor is awarded different assignments, but likely to have remained within the same organization. In terms of the organization, 77 per cent work in medium to large companies (500 or more employees). Their distribution across the three sectors is that most are predominantly from manufacturing (60 per cent), 10 per cent are from retail and 30 per cent are from the services sector.

The policy maker

Three separate characteristics emerge (through factor analysis) which portray the underlying attitudes and styles of management of the policy maker, namely being disciplined, being focused and being communicative, which is identified as involving the following elements:

Disciplined	*Focused*	*Communicative*
• Rules oriented	• Team oriented	• Satisfied
• Structured	• Systems oriented	• Stretched
• Details oriented	• Problem centred	• Well informed
• Relate to those with similar values	• Cross-check alternatives	• Listening oriented
		• Clear
		• Committed
		• Respected
		• Tolerant
		• Valued

Particularly prevalent is the need to be disciplined and systematic. The policy maker, in order to promote a well-structured working environment, is identified as procedures oriented, attentive to details, responsive to rules and discipline. Clarity in terms of ways of working is uppermost in the policy maker's mind, as for them, effectiveness of performance is enhanced if people are clear as to the accountabilities and responsibilities they face in their role. The policy maker is a person who creates clear job boundaries and promotes clear goals. The focus on structure and order is driven by the belief that success at a personal and organizational level is driven by being disciplined on tasks.

In order to action such values, policy makers exhibit considerable respect for command. The same degree of respect is shown towards the procedures and systems applied in the organization, as these are considered the fundamentals which hold the organization together. At a personal level, the policy maker is identified as flexible and positively responsive to people in the organization.

Policy makers consider themselves as satisfied with their work circumstances, and stretched in terms of being challenged in the job. Equally, they display high commitment to the organization. The policy maker seems able to combine focus and discipline with a positive inclination to effectively interact with others. One example of effective interpersonal skills is that the policy maker is rated by others as listening oriented. Further, the individual is seen by colleagues as well informed, viewed as accepting of others and considered as tolerant and approachable.

In terms of overall impact, the policy maker is rated high by colleagues in terms of sharing, being co-operative and being helpful. Their contribution to the organization is appreciated, as is the manner with which they have addressed the issues and challenges they face.

The business driver

Business drivers are identified as portraying a strong results orientation by being:

- Challenging
- Promoting follow through
- Systematic
- Committed to profitability
- Self-directing
- Disciplined
- Disliking interference
- Feedback oriented
- Structured
- Team oriented
- Robust
- Black and white
- Communicative through briefings

Business drivers are motivated by a need for challenge. They are self-directing, independently minded and capable of taking the more unpleasant decisions. They are identified as robust in responding to strain and pressure. They tend to see issues in more black and white terms, which is strongly epitomized by the fact that they consider that there is a right and a wrong way of addressing challenges. Their independence is especially displayed in a dislike of unwelcome interventions, which they would consider as interference in the discharge of their responsibilities.

Self-reliance is coupled with being disciplined and systematic. They highlight that effectiveness of performance can only be truly achieved by being structured and disciplined as a matter of daily practice. The same philosophy is utilized to promote effectiveness of communication. Business drivers insist on being regularly briefed concerning new and existing initiatives. Equally, they demand ever-greater attention to systematic follow through on decisions made.

The discipline applied to communication is coupled with an attentiveness to the quality of managerial relationships. For business drivers, being effective at communication requires a sensitivity to feedback. Making themselves available for comment is central to generating an environment whereby staff and management would feel comfortable to offer their views as to how improvements in the work environment could be achieved. The vehicle for achieving a more open environment is through teams. Business drivers consider themselves team oriented, attempting to promote collegiate relationships so as to achieve a high-quality level of dialogue. Encouraging group cohesion is viewed as a necessary aspect of work-directed behaviour.

Further, with business drivers, as was the case for the policy makers, personal satisfaction and openness of relationships are viewed as necessary to achievement. Hence, for business drivers, commitment to making the organization profitable involves the application of task-related skills, clarity of decision making, a structured and disciplined approach to undertaking tasks of work, in conjunction with more open, team-oriented relationships, recognizing however, that team relationships are secondary to results. For the business driver, task achievement and organizational success are paramount. The flexibility of style portrayed is a 'lever' to achieve those ends.

The implementor

The implementor is identified as disciplined, as conscious of following through on decisions made, as consensus oriented and as working towards generating a stimulating working environment. Each of these aspects is identified as involving the following elements:

Order

- Discipline
- Satisfied
- Respect tradition
- Respect rules
- Procedures oriented
- Team oriented
- Structured

Follow through

- Encourages follow through
- Encourages dialogue
- Accessible

Consensus

- Shares
- Communicates openly
- Respect for protocol
- Tolerant of command
- Cross-checks

Working environment

- Responsive
- Change oriented
- Committed
- Supportive of system of controls
- Tolerant
- Positive
- Job-related challenge

The key characteristics of being a manager whose focus is on implementing strategy, is the need for being structured and disciplined in the undertaking of one's daily workload. Equally, it is important to follow established procedures in order to ensure consistency of application. Such practice could only be effectively applied if respect for both existing rules and the traditions of the organization are displayed. As a part of being disciplined, team work is considered important in order to promote understanding and co-operation. In fact, it is considered that constantly encouraging group cohesion is fundamental to engendering positive and stimulating relationships. Coupled with being satisfied with one's job, the implementor considers that success is achieved by having a management that is well disciplined.

Implementor-oriented managers are equally conscious of follow through on key decisions, emphasizing the need for personal discipline and being systematic in application. In addition, openness of dialogue and creating an environment where work problems can be discussed, are considered as important as being personally rigorous. As a part of generating positive work relationships, being accessible as a senior manager is seen as a necessary condition.

Underlying the discipline and application is a strongly held belief that openness of communication is considered vital. Creating a climate where people feel they can effectively work together is considered fundamental. For the implementor, it is important for staff and management to feel that they can share their work problems. In order to achieve positive levels of communication, checking out plans with colleagues and subordinates in order to encourage greater understanding and sharing of work-related issues, is pursued. Further, the implementor considers it important to promote an image of a sensitive and responsive management, so that lower-level management hold top management and the command structure of the organization in respect. As a part of promoting an image of a more cohesive organization, the implementor feels it important that they and their staff display a respect for protocol in the way official engagements and formal relationships are managed.

Equally, a positive attitude to the job is portrayed. The implementor feels that their work affords a stretching and challenging experience. Satisfaction with the organization extends to being committed to it, as portrayed in the positive attitude they display towards the systems and controls in the organization. Further, implementors identify themselves as responsive to the opinions of others and work towards establishing a culture at the top of the organization of tolerance amongst senior managers.

Overall, the implementor is concerned with promoting a positive working environment in the organization. It is their belief that with greater encouragement, staff and management will become more self-confident. In this way, those in the organization are more likely to raise personal, task-related and organizational issues that require attention. For the implementor, attaining high levels of consensus is an end in itself. In contrast, for the policy maker, effectiveness of communication is crucial to promoting clear direction, whereas for the business driver, openness is one lever for goal attainment.

Organizational performance characteristics

From the initial unstructured interviews, particular aspects of organizational performance are identified. For example, the issues raised covered internal organizational performance concerns such as the motivation and performance of employees, management of costs, structuring of organization, effectiveness of interfacing, quality of products and services, current product/services portfolio and viability of sales and marketing practice. Equally, externally oriented matters were discussed, such as competitive advantage and its sustenance, insights as to the behaviour and intents of competitors, quality of service to clients, responding to feedback from the marketplace, as well as other factors. Issues such as these were included in the Japanese Executive Competencies questionnaire as single items. Respondents were asked to identify those items that in their opinion were relevant to the current and future performance of their organization. The single items identified were analysed, with five key factors emerging.

Two organizational performance factors are identified by the Japanese respondents, namely, quality of top-team relationships and harmony. Four factors from the European respondents emerge, namely, quality of top team relationships, performance motivation, market responsiveness and strategic orientation. The Japanese and European respondents share the same factor concerning quality of relationships within the top team.

Top team relationships (Europe/Japan)

Effectively managed relationships within the top team requires being:

- Understanding of each other
- Trusting of each other
- Able to discuss sensitive issues
- Easy to talk to as people
- Able to implement decisions jointly made
- Able to address long- and short-term issues

Both the European and Japanese senior managers consider that in order for senior management to perform effectively as a team, the quality of dialogue amongst the members of the team needs to be open, so as to allow for full examination of the issues facing the organization. The respondents consider that it is imperative for the team members to have the confidence in each other to discuss sensitive issues of an individual, departmental or organizational nature, that impact on the performance of the company. In order to create an environment where confidence and openness of dialogue are possible, the levels of trust amongst the team members are considered as needing to be high. One element for enhancing levels of trust is for the relevant senior managers to understand each other as people. Through understanding each other, through appreciating the strengths and weaknesses of each other's style(s) and through recognizing the challenges and pressures each senior manager faces in terms of their accountabilities and responsibilities in role, comments can be more sensitively made according to the issues facing each colleague. Such a working environment allows for a level of comfort in senior management relationships to act as a springboard for a fuller exploration of the challenges facing the organization.

Two key issues, in particular, are identified by both senior Japanese and European leaders, as crucial elements to team working, namely the addressing of long- and short-term issues and the confidence that decisions made in meetings will be jointly implemented. The Cranfield survey identified no particular distinction emerging between working on longer- on shorter-term objectives. In essence, both sets of objectives are considered as necessary to address, virtually simultaneously. Discussing longer-term issues may be experienced as stimulating, as conversation may focus more on concepts, priorities and options. Discussing shorter-term issues may be experienced as more sensitive, as the performance of senior colleagues and/or their departments/functions may come under scrutiny. Evolving a maturity of relationship is important to be able to discuss both ends of the spectrum.

Quality of dialogue in the meeting influences the effectiveness of decision implementation. Dysfunctional team behaviour occurs when, on having discussed and decided on ways forward, each senior manager only implements what personally suits, after the meeting. Such behaviour signifies no meaningful commitment to cabinet responsibility or to the decision-making processes amongst the senior management of the organization. Growing a sense of shared responsibility within senior management so that the decisions made are jointly implemented, requires having engendered a positively oriented team environment.

Harmony (Japan)

The Japanese respondents identify harmony as an important issue influencing senior managerial relationships. Harmony is identified as involving the following elements:

- Enhancing employee morale
- Stimulating greater trust
- Improving performance from employees
- Enhancing internal organizational relationships

Particularly relevant to the Japanese respondents is the concept of harmonious relationships within the work situation. Harmony involves creating an environment whereby enhancing employee morale occurs naturally. As a result, people within the organization are likely to be more trusting of each other and of their leadership. Within a culture of improved morale and greater trust, it is considered that performance from employees will naturally improve as pride in the workplace increases. As motivation and relationships improve at the individual level, then greater attention and care is likely to be given to the quality of interfacing between departments and functions.

Performance motivation (Europe)

The European respondents identify that motivating people to improve performance involves:

- Enhancing employee morale
- Stimulating greater trust
- Having fewer people leaving the organization
- Having fewer inaccurate commitments made internally
- Improving performance from employees
- Generating improved internal organizational relationships

Positive working relationships are equally important to the European respondents but greater emphasis is placed on promoting a positive attitude to work-related performance than quality of relationships in their own right. As with the Japanese respondents, creating a stimulating environment whereby effective working relationships are considered as important, is a priority for the Europeans. Through improved working relationships, greater trust can be achieved between the levels of management and horizontally across the organization. Being more stimulated in the workplace is seen to lead to improved performance from employees. Improvements in morale and quality of working environment are identified by the Europeans as reducing employee turnover. Equally, as staff and management feel more positive about the organization, it is likely that fewer inaccurate commitments are going to be made between functions/departments in the organization and between managers and their staff. The overall result is that improved internal organizational relationships are likely to emerge.

Market responsiveness (Europe)

The European respondents identify that being responsive to the market-place involves:

- Discussions concerning competitor impact
- Being able to handle competitors
- Focusing on key customer groups
- Being committed to clients
- Being responsive to new initiatives
- Providing better relationships
- Being able to deliver goods/services
- Becoming profitable through effective sales/marketing

For the European respondents, a key measure of organizational performance is being market responsive. Particularly pertinent is the quality of dialogue inside the organization concerning developments in the marketplace. The openness and honesty of discussion amongst managers within the organization concerning competitor impact is viewed as vital in order to enhance understanding of opportunities within the markets. Certain conversation is likely to focus on the ability of staff and management to respond to competitors, which is one side of the equation. The other side is responsiveness to customers. A particular concern of the Europeans is the degree to which managers are focused to respond to the requirements of key customer groups. Appreciating the varying needs and demands of the organization's customer base is necessary in order to fulfil existing and future commitments to clients. Equally, it is considered that being market responsive requires that attention needs to be given to the effectiveness of service delivery.

By attending to internal and external organizational requirements, the ability of staff and management to respond to new initiatives is likely to be more efficient. As a result, improved external relationships are likely to follow. Overall, sensitivity to interfaces internally and responsiveness to the markets externally, provide for the foundation to the effective application of sales and marketing. In effect, profitability through sales and marketing is viewed as the result of effective internal and external interface management.

Strategic orientation (Europe)

The European respondents identify that being strategic requires examining:

- Issues affecting the long term
- The future of the company
- The quality of products/services
- Cost management
- The product/service portfolio

The European respondents identify particular perspectives, which for them are prime strategic considerations, and which they consider makes an impact on the longer-term viability of the company. The degree to which management are aware of the issues affecting the longer-term prospects of the organization, and thereby have formed a view as to how future developments are likely to affect the company, are highlighted as important elements of strategy generation. Equally, issues pertaining to the quality of the current range of products/services and the effectiveness of cost management within the organization are viewed as considerations of strategy.

Impact of Japanese leaders

Having identified the different characteristics of Japanese leaders, and the people and organization-related performance challenges both the Japanese and European respondents consider important to address, cross-correlation analysis is undertaken examining the relationship between leadership and performance. The following results highlight the likely impact Japanese managers will have within Japanese organizations and in holding senior expatriate positions, in a country of European staff and management (Table 3.5).

Impact of the policy maker

The orientation to effectiveness of communication is rated as having a positive impact by the majority of the country managers in the sample. Being attentive to good communication is rated as enhancing team identity, team purpose and cohesion amongst team members by the Japanese respondents. The British, Irish, Germans, Swedes, Spanish and Austrians identify that Japanese leaders who are effective at communication are likely to positively impact on team relationships, the motivation of staff and management to improve performance, the responsiveness of staff and management to be sensitive to market and customer requirement, and on the overall awareness of employees concerning strategic issues and the future development of the company.

The discipline element of the policy maker's style is identified by the British respondents as having a positive contribution to helping managers be more market responsive. In contrast, the French respondents identify the application of discipline as counter-productive in terms of assisting French managers to focus on strategic issues. Equally, the Spanish and Austrians find the discipline-oriented Japanese manager as unhelpful in addressing organizational performance issues. Specifically, the Spanish indicate that motivation to perform, being market responsive and being more strategically aware are hindered with the

Table 3.5 Effectiveness of Japanese leaders

Manager	Japan Team	Japan Harmony	UK Team	UK Perf. motiv.	UK Market resp.	UK Strat.	France Team	France Perf. motiv.	France Market resp.	France Strat.	Ireland Team	Ireland Perf. motiv.	Ireland Market resp.	Ireland Strat.	Germany Team	Germany Perf. motiv.	Germany Market resp.	Germany Strat.
Policy makers																		
Communicate	**		**	**	**	**		**				**	*	**	**	**		**
Discipline					*					—*								**
Focus	*		**	**		**						*						
Business drivers																		
Results oriented	**	—*				—*						—*						
Implementors																		
Order							*											
Work environment	**		**	**	**	**	**	**		**	**	**	**	**		**	**	
Follow through	**			**		**		*					—*					
Consensus	*		**	**		**		*		*								

Manager	Japan Team	Japan Harmony	Sweden Team	Sweden Perf. motiv.	Sweden Market resp.	Sweden Strat.	Spain Team	Spain Perf. motiv.	Spain Market resp.	Spain Strat.	Austria Team	Austria Perf. motiv.	Austria Market resp.	Austria Strat.	Finland Team	Finland Perf. motiv.	Finland Market resp.	Finland Strat.
Policy makers																		
Communicate	**		**	**	**	**	**	**	**	**	**	**	**	**				
Discipline								—*	—**	—*		—**		—*				
Focus	*		**				**	**	*	*	**	**	*	*			*	
Business drivers																		
Results oriented	**	—*					—**	—**	—**	—**		—**		—**				
Implementors																		
Order					—**		—**	—*	—**	—*		—*		—*				
Work environment	**		**	**			**	**	**	**	**	**	**	**			*	
Follow through	**			**					—**	—**		**		—**				*
Consensus	*						**	**	—**	**		**		**				

Notes: Team: team relations. perf. motiv: motivation to perform. market resp.: responsiveness to markets. strat.: strategic orientation. *: significant at the 05 level. **: significant at the 01 level. —: negative correlation application of a disciplined approach to management. The Austrians indicate that team relationships and performance motivation are negatively affected through the application of discipline.

Japanese leaders that are focused are considered by the Japanese respondents as enhancing team relationships. Similarly, the British, Spanish and Austrians consider that a Japanese leader with a focused approach provides a positive impact on organizational performance. In particular, the British consider that team relationships, motivation to perform and the awareness of managers concerning strategic issues are improved through the use of a focused style of management. Equally positive sentiments are expressed by both the Spanish and Austrians who consider that team relations, motivation to perform, being market responsive and being more strategically aware, are enhanced through the application of a focused approach to managing. In addition, the Irish respondents consider that motivation to perform improves and for the Swedes and Finns, team relations improve, through the application of a focused style.

Impact of the business driver

The results-oriented style of the business driver is identified by the Japanese respondents as a positive influence in terms of promoting effective team relationships. However, in terms of promoting harmony within the organization, being results-oriented is viewed by the Japanese respondents as having a negative effect.

As far as the European respondents are concerned, being results-oriented is seen not to have any particular significant impact other than on specific organizational performance measures in particular countries. The British and Irish respondents consider that Japanese leaders who are too results-oriented are likely to have a more negative impact on staff and management's motivation to perform in their job. The Spanish respondents highlight that those Japanese top managers leading a Spanish management and workforce displaying a results-oriented style, are likely to have a negative influence on team relationships, the motivation of people to perform, the market responsiveness of staff and management and the strategic orientation and awareness of the management in the organization. The Austrians indicate a negative impact on their employees in terms of worsening team relationships and a reduction in staff and management's motivation to perform.

Impact of the implementor

The orientation towards being ordered and systematic is identified as having a significant impact on the French, Spanish and Austrian respondents. The French consider that being ordered and protocol-driven has a positive effect on team relationships amongst French managers. In contrast, the Spanish consider an ordered style as having a counter-productive impact on team relationships, performance motivation, being market responsive and having strategic awareness. The Austrians consider that Japanese leaders who apply an ordered work approach have a negative effect on team relationships and the motivation of staff and management to perform.

However, generating a working environment where staff and management are satisfied with their organization stimulates far more positive results. The Japanese respondents consider that an organizational environment which staff and management find satisfactory has a positive impact on team relationships. The British, Irish, Swedish, Spanish and Austrian respondents consider that satisfaction with one's working environment enhances team relationships, increases people's motivation to perform, helps staff and management to be more market responsive and promotes a greater willingness to comprehend the strategic challenges facing the organization. The French respondents highlight a positive impact on team relationships, staff and management performance motivation and stimulating greater strategic awareness amongst management. The German respondents indicate that with improved levels of satisfaction within the organization, team relationships and the performance motivation of staff and management are likely to improve. The Finnish respondents display a similar positive inclination, highlighting improvements in team relationships and greater focus on market-related challenges.

Being disciplined at follow-through is identified by the Japanese respondents as having a positive influence on team relationships. The French consider that effectiveness at follow-through has a positive effect on the motivation to perform on French staff and management. The Swedes, in keeping with the French, consider that Japanese applying follow-through is likely to improve the motivation of staff and management. In contrast, the Spanish consider that effectiveness of follow-through is likely to be counter-productive with Spanish staff and management in terms of being market responsive or more strategically oriented. The Irish, equally, consider that Japanese managers who apply a follow-through style are more likely to demotivate Irish staff and management.

A consensus building style of systematically working with others, sharing problems and promoting more open communication is considered by certain of the respondents as beneficial to team relationships. The British respondents consider that Japanese managers who apply a consensus-oriented approach have a positive impact on team relationships, performance motivation and strategic awareness. The French and Spaniards rate consensus-oriented management as having a positive influence on the performance motivation and the strategic awareness of their staff and management, while the Swedes highlight a positive correlation with performance motivation. The Finns indicate a positive correlation between a consensus style and the enhancing of team relationships.

SUMMARY

- The Japanese in comparison to the European respondents, with the exception of the Swedish, identify the least degree of divergence of fundamentally different views concerning the future direction of their organization. In effect, the Japanese display the highest degree of agreement on vision and strategic direction.
- The Japanese in comparison to the other European respondents, identify the highest level of inability to address known sensitive issues that exist within their organization. The Japanese are the most likely to allow known and sensitive problems to continue without them being addressed.
- The Japanese in comparison to the other European respondents, consider their top managers and the general managers below to be more trusting of each other. Hence, Japanese managers are more likely to recognize and capitalize on each other's strengths.
- Three styles of business leadership amongst the Japanese respondents are identified, from those managers that occupy a policy-making role, from those that are results-driven and from those that are concerned with the implementation of strategy. Such differences of attitude and behaviour reflect differences of seniority, length of time in company and length of time in job. Basically, those longer in the organization and more senior are likely to adopt a more consensus-oriented approach rather than a more businesslike short-term approach.
- Particular elements of each of the Japanese leadership styles are identified as having a positive impact on Japanese and European managers, namely, being communicative, being focused and attempting to create an environment whereby staff and management are satisfied with their organization.
- The consensus-oriented approach, although recognized as having a positive impact on Japanese and European managers, is considered as having less impact than effectively managed approaches to communication, being focused and nurturing an organizational environment with which staff and management can positively identify.
- The results-oriented approach is identified as having more of a negative impact on Japanese and European managers.

NOTES

1 Studies of top managers have tended to fall into two categories: those that focus job role and organization-related criteria (Mintzberg 1973; Stewart 1982; van Wolferen 1989) or an examination of the attributes of individuals in terms of behavioural, attitudinal or deeper personality dimensions (Bennis and Nanus 1985; Kotter 1982; Margerison and Lewis 1983; Kouzes and Posner 1993). Few studies of Japanese managers concentrate on job- or role-related issues, other than comparative studies of US and Japanese CEOs (Chief Executive Officers) (Suzuki 1986) the age of CEOs (Zimmerman 1985) and differences in how US and Japanese CEOs spend their time (Kudo, Tachikawa and Suzuki 1988). Far greater emphasis is placed on value and attitudinal differences (Mauser and Stewart 1982; Crump 1989a), with certain authors concluding that Japanese managers are better equipped to manage Western-based employees (Ishida 1986; Johnson 1988). Shimizu's (1992) analysis of 10,000 Japanese companies and interviews with 150 Japanese CEOs emphasizes networking as a key aspect of leadership in Japanese companies. The CEO exerts influence over the board members through the process of *Kashi/ Kari*, in effect the undertaking of personal favours on behalf of fellow directors who in turn feel beholden to the individual and obliged to support the CEOs' views and decisions. The point is supported by Zimmerman (1985) who considers that leadership in Japan is focused on achieving consensus within groups, through outward humility, *totemae*, in order to attain harmony, *wa*.

 However, Guptara (1994) emphasizes the stereotypic nature of such perceptions, arguing that they fail to explain the mechanics of Japanese leadership. This view is supported by the Cranfield researchers, whose initial and intensive case analyses in European organizations of the key influences which impact on the decision-forming dialogue, the making of decisions and decision implementation processes, strongly suggests that both personal characteristics and job/role considerations need to be taken into account (Kakabadse 1991a).

 In promoting this theme, the original and insightful work of Professor Elliot Jaques (Jaques 1951) examining different cultures within the workplace, provides the conceptual bridge between individual behaviours and role requirements. Crucial to the work of Jaques is the concept of *discretion*. The discretionary element of role refers to the choices the role incumbent needs to make in order to provide shape and identity to their role and that part of the organization for which the person is accountable. The contrast to the discretionary element of role is the prescriptive side, namely the structured part, which is pre-determined and which drives the individual's behaviour. In effect, the prescriptive part of a manager's job is that part over which the manager has little choice, other than to undertake the duties that are required of the person. Professor Paul Evans (Evans 1994) of the International Business School of Insead (Paris) draws similar distinctions when he refers to the manager's job as a split between the leadership elements (discretionary) and the managerial elements (prescriptive). Such distinctions is particularly pertinent, as providing leadership for stakeholder value is likely to make considerable demand on the discretionary elements of a senior manager's role.

2 CEO (Chief Executive Officer); ED (Executive Director); MD (Managing Director); GM (General Manager).

3 We acknowledge the permission given by Professor Shaun Tyson to publish contents of one of our papers emanating from this research in Tyson (1995) *Strategic Prospects for H.R.M.*, in this book.

Chapter 4

Japanese managerial style: differences by sector

We differentiate ourselves from other companies by providing reliability and speed by which we respond to our customers' calls, which
of course amounts to quality of service. Because our company is new
. . . we only began to recruit graduates from university in 1970, so if
they come through internal promotion, they are just beginning to
reach the board level. It is still a very young company.

(Chairman, a company in the Japanese service industry)

KEY ISSUES

Top Japanese managers from the three sectors of manufacturing, retail
and services are represented. A sample of 402 top manufacturing managers represent consumer and industrial manufacturing. A sample of
ninety-seven top retail managers represent wholesale and retail organizations. A sample of 262 top services managers represent distribution,
financial services, health care and consulting, information, also leisure
services organizations.

Key differences between the sectors are identified. Senior managers
from the service sector are identified as more managerially capable and
displaying a more positive attitude to their organization. Interestingly, it
is the managers from the service sector that show greater concern for
improving service quality than managers from the other two sectors.

Demographics

The age profile of senior managers in the retail sector is younger than the
senior managers in the manufacturing and services sectors. Of senior
managers, 49 per cent in retail fall into the age band 46–55 years, whereas
65 per cent of senior managers in manufacturing and 62 per cent of
managers in services fall into the age band of 55-plus years (Table 4.1).

Further, senior managers in the manufacturing sector indicate that
they have been employed longest in the same company. Of senior man-

agers, 64 per cent from manufacturing have been with the same company for over twenty years, whereas 49 per cent from retail and 45 per cent from services indicate they have remained in the same company for over twenty years. Noteworthy is that 26 per cent of senior managers from service organizations have been in the company for up to only four years, which is more than double the percentage for the other two sectors. Such a phenomenon could be explained by the fact that companies from the services and retail sector are relatively new in comparison to companies from the manufacturing sector. In addition, respondents from the manufacturing and services sectors highlight that the jobs of managers of all grades are more structured and clearly defined in terms of areas of responsibility and accountability, than the job of managers from the retail sector.

Table 4.1 Differences across sectors (Japan): demographics

Significant difference (chi square)	Manufacturing	Retail	Services
Age		<55	
Years in company	>20		
Job definition	**		**

Note: Significant at the 01 level

Management style

Senior managers from retail and services consider themselves as more disciplined in administration and day-to-day management (Table 4.2). Further, they consider that such discipline is fundamental to success. In terms of adherence to rules, senior managers from services and manufacturing consider their organizations as more rule bound.

Table 4.2 Differences across sectors (Japan): management style

Significant differences (chi square)	Manufacturing	Retail	Services
Disciplined		**	**
Rule bound	**		**
Responsive to pressure	**		**
Feedback oriented			**

Note: ** Significant at the 01 level

However, in responding to strain and pressure, senior managers from the manufacturing and services sectors consider themselves and their subordinates as more capable of managing such contingencies. Finally, in terms of communication and feedback, senior managers from service organizations indicate that they receive a higher-quality feedback from staff and management. In particular, being kept informed of progress on new initiatives is highlighted as an area of excellence.

Attitudes to the company

Two issues are identified, the attitudes displayed towards the systems and controls in the company and the experience of managers towards change, that have taken place in the company (Table 4.3). Senior managers from manufacturing are more likely to consider that the systems and controls in the company are a hindrance to them, whereas the managers from retail and service project a more positive attitude.

Table 4.3 Differences across sectors (Japan): attitudes to company

Significant differences (chi square)	Manufacturing	Retail	Services
Systems and controls		**	**
Change			**

Note: ** Significant at the 01 level

The senior managers from service organizations indicate a more positive response to the changes experienced in their organization. The senior managers from manufacturing and retail indicate that their company has been misguided about certain of the changes that have taken place.

Issues requiring attention

People-related issues requiring attention are identified as key by the senior managers from manufacturing and service organizations (Table 4.4 overleaf). Further, nurturing senior manager relationships in order to effectively implement policy is considered as crucial by the respondents from manufacturing and services but requiring greater attention. The reason is that the relationships amongst senior managers are considered as less cohesive in organizations from these sectors. Equally, being responsive to staff and management relationships, in general, is also considered as a concern. However, the senior managers from the retail sector consider that they are more likely to face problems with the performance of particular managers than staff and managerial relationships in general.

The senior managers from retail identify that they have greater

Table 4.4 Differences across sectors (Japan): issues requiring attention

Significant differences (chi square)	Manufacturing	Retail	Services
Managing top team	**		**
Relationships	**		**
Manager performance		**	
Competitor analysis		**	
Addressing the long term		**	
Quality of products/services			**

Note: ** Significant at the 01 level

strategic concerns to address in their organizations. In particular, they highlight competitor analysis and confront long-term issues more as concerns than the managers from the other two sectors. It is considered that the line managers in retail organizations pay less attention to the impact of their competitors than the line managers from manufacturing and services. Hence, there exists less of an urgency to debate and address issues concerning medium- to long-term strategy, by management. Quality is identified as an area of significant difference by the respondent from the three sectors. The senior managers from services indicate that they have more quality issues to address than the respondents from the other two sectors.

SUMMARY

Three sectors (Japan)

- Senior managers in retail organizations are identified as younger than the managers in comparable positions in manufacturing and service organizations.
- Managers in manufacturing organizations have remained longer within the same company than managers from retail and service organizations.
- Managers from service organizations are identified as being more positive in terms of their managerial style, especially in terms of being disciplined, being feedback oriented, being communicative and being responsive to pressure, than the respondents from manufacturing and retail organizations.
- The senior managers from services highlight a more positive response to the systems, administration and control mechanisms in

their organizations and to the changes that have taken place in their organizations, than the managers from manufacturing and retail.

- The senior managers from manufacturing and service organizations consider that the overall performance of their staff and management is worthy of further attention in order to enhance improvement. Their concerns would include improving functional performance as well as managerial and leadership performance, in terms of managing relationships and internal communications.

- Broader strategic concerns are identified as requiring more attention by the managers from the retail sector. The complex wholesale–retail channel to market chain is seen as expensive and unwieldy and the three years of 1991–4 witnessed a drop in consumer spending. Pricing and internal costs are considered as fundamental issues which need confronting.

- Quality of service is identified as more of a concern by the senior managers from service organizations than by the respondents from the retail and manufacturing sectors.

Chapter 5

International management styles: country/sector comparison – Japan/Europe

Working towards a fully unified and integrated European company, it is evident from our experience that success depends not only on investment in machines but also in people – caring about them, training them and motivating them by helping them to realize their full potential.

(A. Nakagawa, ex-President, Sumitomo Rubber Europe)

KEY ISSUES

A cross-country/sector comparison spread throughout eight European countries and Japan of differences and similarities over issues of organization, managerial and leadership styles and strategic and operational challenges is presented. The analysis includes 1,558 senior managers from the manufacturing sector, 362 senior managers from the retail sector and 1,199 from the services sector.

The fundamental learning point is that the Japanese are no better or worse than their European counterparts. But three areas of difference distinguish the Japanese from the Europeans, namely that, role-for-role equivalents, Japanese senior managers are identified as older, and that the Japanese display a significantly higher level of satisfaction with their work than do the Europeans. Further, the Japanese also seem to be more mature in their response to managing challenges of a broader general management nature. From there on, differences of organization, management and leadership style and issues of strategy and operational management, vary either by country or by sector. Both the Japanese and European economies have reached the stage of maturity and, in terms of organization and management, display similar challenges and concerns. Bearing in mind the tensions of leadership philosophy and style identified in Chapter 3, namely over addressing sensitive concerns and the differences between policy makers and business drivers, it would be interesting to observe whether the more positive response to addressing general management issues would continue to survive.

Nine areas of significant difference have emerged: issues of demography, work satisfaction, orientation towards being specialist, independence orientation, attitudes towards the company, effectiveness of follow-through, management style, top team dynamics and areas requiring attention within the company.

MANUFACTURING SECTOR: RESULTS

Demographics

Senior managers of Japanese companies are significantly older (over 55 years) than managers in comparable positions in companies in the eight European countries (Table 5.1). A significant proportion of senior managers in French, Irish, German and Spanish companies are under 46 years. In terms of years in job, a significant proportion of senior Japanese managers report that they are less than a year in their current position whereas Spanish senior managers report that they have remained longest in the same job. In contrast, Japanese managers report they remain longest in the same company (over twenty years), whereas British, French, Swedish and Austrian managers highlight their mobility more than the other respondents, in that they indicate they have been in their company for a period of under four years.

Other than the Japanese and Swedish senior managers, the remaining respondents highlight that managers' jobs are relatively clearly defined in terms of the accountabilities and responsibilities in their role. Differences are highlighted in terms of communication of objectives. Japanese and British senior managers consider that functional objectives are clearly communicated. As far as corporate objectives are concerned, providing direction from a corporate centre is considered as effectively undertaken by Japanese, French, Irish, German and Swedish senior managers.

Work satisfaction

All but the French senior managers indicate high levels of satisfaction with their current jobs (Table 5.2). French senior managers are the only group that significantly indicate that they wish to leave their jobs. Further, French and Swedish senior managers report higher levels of stress than the other respondents. French senior managers report that their jobs are not clearly understood by their colleagues. Equally, the French report that they display the least need for helping to make their colleagues aware of the nature and demands of their own jobs.

Table 5.1 Demographics (manufacturing)

Issues		Significant difference (chi square)						
	Japan	UK	France	Ireland	Germany	Sweden	Spain	Austria
Age	>55		<46	<46	<46		<46	
Job years	<1						>10	
Company years	>20	<4	<4			<4		<4
Job definition		**	**	**	**		**	**
Functional objectives	**	**						
Corporate objectives	**		**	**	**	**		

Note: ** Significant at the 01 level

Table 5.2 Work satisfaction (manufacturing)

Issues	Japan	UK	France	Ireland	Germany	Sweden	Spain	Austria
					Significant difference (chi square)			
Job satisfaction	**	**		**	**	**	**	**
Stress			**			**		
Job clarity	**	**		**	**	**	**	**
Growth opportunities	**	**			**			**
Commitment	**	**	**	**		**	**	**
Over-sensitive		**	**	**	**	**	**	**
Leave job			**					

Note: ** Significant at the 01 level

Japanese, British, German and Austrian senior managers report higher levels of opportunity for growth and development in the jobs of managers. In contrast, French senior managers consider their jobs to be limiting and lacking in stimulation. Irish, Swedish and Spanish recognize their jobs as constraining but not to the same degree as reported by French senior managers.

Other than Japanese senior managers, the remaining respondents report that they can be over-sensitive to the opinions that others hold of them. Such opinions are highlighted as influencing the behaviour and attitudes of the senior managers concerned.

Being specialist

French, German and Austrian senior managers report that their greatest work satisfaction comes from the technical/specialist side of their job (Table 5.3). French senior managers further report that they communicate easier with others from a similar technical background. In fact, the French respondents express enthusiasm and satisfaction at assisting others from a similar professional background to understand the technical aspects of their job.

French, Irish, German, Spanish and Austrian senior managers report that they and their managers in the company are as much valued for their technical expertise as for their managerial skills. In keeping with the orientation towards expertise, British, Irish, German, Spanish and Austrian senior managers report that they value being a member of a profession. Japanese and Swedish senior managers indicate no significant orientation towards technical and/or job-related specialisms.

Independence

British, French and Irish senior managers display the highest need for self-determination (Table 5.4). They indicate that they like being in a position where others do not have control over them. Further, French, German and Austrian managers are likely to feel resentment at being told what to do and indicate that they are likely to display such sentiments in the work situation.

Apart from Swedish managers, the remaining respondents report that they do not like others to interfere in their work domain. Japanese, British, French, Irish and Spanish senior managers report that on task-related issues they essentially wish to do things their way. The British, Irish and Spanish, in particular, display the highest needs for desiring the flexibility to determine workloads and activities as they consider appropriate.

For the Japanese, displaying a need for independence in terms of

Table 5.3 Specialist orientation (manufacturing)

Issues	Japan	UK	Significant difference (chi square)					
			France	Ireland	Germany	Sweden	Spain	Austria
Specialist satisfaction			**		**			**
Technical communication			**					
Expertise			**	**	**		**	**
Professional membership		**		**	**		**	**

Note: ** Significant at the 01 level

Table 5.4 Independence orientation (manufacturing)

Issues	Japan	UK	France	Ireland	Germany	Sweden	Spain	Austria
					Significant difference (chi square)			
Self-determination		**	**	**				
Work determination		**		**			**	
Resentment of control			**		**			**
Dislike interference	**	**	**	**	**		**	**
Get own way	**	**	**	**			**	
Being the boss		**	**	**	**	**	**	**

Note: ** Significant at the 01 level

determination of tasks does not extend to being seen to be in control. The respondents from the European countries highlight that being recognized and respected as the 'boss' is motivating. Being in control is identified as insignificant by the Japanese respondents.

Attitudes to the company

Japanese, French, German, Swedish, Spanish and Austrian senior managers report a positive attitude to the financial controls utilized in their companies (Table 5.5). In contrast, British and Irish senior managers indicate wastage in their companies due to poor financial controls. Japanese, British, Irish, Swedish, Spanish and Austrian senior managers report greater levels of stability in managers' jobs. Managers do not feel that they experience too rapid or unwarranted disruption and change which would limit the effectiveness of their performance in their job. However, the French and Germans highlight that their managers are moved on to different jobs too quickly. Japanese, French, Irish and Spanish senior managers report higher levels of respect for the traditions of their company. A different perspective is taken by the British, German, Swedish and Austrian respondents who indicate that tradition is not sacrosanct when change is deemed necessary.

However, whatever the attitude to tradition, the British, French, Swedish and Austrian managers report a positive attitude to change. They indicate that the changes that have taken place in their organizations have been for the best. The Irish and Spanish are more extreme in their comments on change, in that they are more likely to feel that their company has been misguided in many of the changes that have been carried out. Japanese and German respondents are less critical in that they do not see change as unwelcome but feel that some of the changes in their company could have been better managed. Their opinion is that the poor morale of staff resulting from changes that have taken place should have been given greater attention. Despite the attitudes to change, current systems and controls are viewed by Japanese, British, Swedish and Spanish senior managers as valuable and effective. Relationships at departmental level are considered by Japanese, French, Irish, German, Spanish and Austrian senior managers as needing improvement. British and Swedish senior managers report that such relationships require constant attention but are currently reasonably effective.

Follow-through

Japanese, British, Irish, German, Swedish, Spanish and Austrian senior managers highlight that being disciplined, as an aspect of follow-

Table 5.5 Attitudes towards the company (manufacturing)

Issues	Significant difference (chi square)							
	Japan	UK	France	Ireland	Germany	Sweden	Spain	Austria
Financial controls	**		**		**	**	**	**
Job stability	**	**		**		**	**	**
Traditions	**		**	**			**	
System and controls	**	**				**	**	
Change		**	**			**		**
Departmental relationships		**				**		

Note: ** Significant at the 01 level

through, is fundamental to success (Table 5.6). French senior managers feel that this issue is less important. In fact, whereas other respondents report that they like to see their staff and management to be well disciplined, the French indicate that such an attribute is less valued. As far as meetings are concerned, British, German, Swedish and Austrian senior managers indicate that the managers in their organization are more likely to display the necessary levels of discipline and consistency concerning attendance, timekeeping and addressing items on the agenda. Japanese, French, Irish and Spanish senior managers report that their staff and management should be more disciplined at attending and effectively working issues through meetings. The French, in particular, highlight meetings discipline as a problem in that they separately indicated that management meetings are changed or cancelled with little or no notice.

British, French, Irish, Swedish and Spanish senior managers feel it is important to follow established work procedures. In fact, apart from the Swedish managers, setting clear parameters for working and reporting back are seen as important by the senior managers from the remaining countries. More specifically, following established rules is valued by French, German, Spanish and Austrian senior managers. Equally, being disciplined about progress updates is valued by all of the respondents except the Japanese; however, respecting protocol is reported by only Japanese and Swedish managers.

Needing to become more effective at follow-through is considered as necessary by all of the respondents, except the Swedish managers. Particular attention in terms of follow-through on current and new initiatives is considered to require improvement. This is particularly the case for the French and Irish senior managers who report that losing track of new initiatives is commonplace, at both senior and middle-management levels. As far as people management is concerned, Japanese, British, French, Irish, Swedish and Spanish senior managers report that team cohesion requires constant encouragement. In contrast, German and Austrian senior managers report that effectively structuring people's roles is a more significant lever in terms of attaining group cohesion.

Management style

British, Irish, German, Spanish and Austrian senior managers identify themselves as more uncommunicative than the remaining senior managers in the sample (Table 5.7). They consider it takes a substantial amount of time for staff and management to get to know them as people. In contrast, the French are the only group to report that the

Table 5.6 Follow through (manufacturing)

Issues	Japan	UK	France	Ireland	Germany	Sweden	Spain	Austria
					Significant difference (chi square)			
Discipline	**	**		**	**	**	**	**
Meetings discipline		**			**	**		**
Procedures		**	**	**		**	**	
Progress updates		**	**	**	**	**	**	**
Parameters	**	**	**	**	**		**	**
Rule bound			**		**		**	**
Protocol	**					**		
Losing track			**	**				
Attention to follow through						**		
Team cohesion	**	**	**	**		**	**	

Notes: ** Significant at the 01 level

Table 5.7 Management style (manufacturing)

Issues	Japan	UK	France	Ireland	Germany	Sweden	Spain	Austria
Emotionality			**					
Uncommunicative		**		**	**		**	**
Sensitivity	**						**	**
Feedback oriented	**	**		**	**	**		**
Maturity		**	**	**	**	**		**
Accessibility		**	**	**	**	**	**	**
Criticism	**		**	**		**		

Note: ** Significant at the 01 level

staff and management in their organizations think their bosses emotional in their manner of behaviour.

Japanese, Spanish and Austrian senior managers view themselves as sensitive to the views and sentiments of other people. They report that their approach to decision making is to both logically consider options and also be considerate of staff and management's response to the decisions made and their implementation. In terms of inviting feedback, the French and Spanish indicate a greater reluctance to make themselves available to receive comments, especially if the feedback focuses on the style of the manager. Whether through feedback or uninvited comment, Japanese, Irish, Swedish and French senior managers highlight their sensitivity and adverse reaction to criticism. However, all respondents indicate that on issues of task performance, considerable effort is given to encouraging subordinates to discuss their concerns with their manager. The sensitivity reported by the respondents is when feedback is seen to become more of a personal attack.

Other than the Japanese and Spanish senior managers, the remaining senior managers consider that they are seen by their colleagues and subordinates as displaying the necessary maturity required of their position. In terms of personal style, the Japanese senior managers feel that they require further development in making themselves more accessible to their staff. The European senior managers consider themselves as accessible and easy to talk to over work difficulties or more personal issues and problems.

Top team

The levels of trust amongst senior managers in Japanese, British, French and Swedish top teams is rated as high (Table 5.8). Further, Japanese, British, French, Swedish and Austrian senior managers rate the quality of dialogue in their teams as higher than the Irish, German and Spanish senior managers. Particularly highlighted by the Japanese, British, French, Swedish and Austrian respondents is that they more readily enter into discussion of issues of sensitivity, whereas the others report that they are more likely to discuss issues considered as 'safe'. Equally, Japanese, British, Swedish and Austrian senior managers consider themselves as tolerant and accepting of the style of their colleagues as well as being understanding as to the challenges and pressures faced by their colleagues.

With high levels of trust and good-quality dialogue, Japanese, British, French and Swedish senior managers highlight that they implement decisions that have jointly been made within the top team. German and Austrian senior managers report similar findings, but attribute consistency of decision implementation to adherence to a systematic

Table 5.8 Top team (manufacturing)

Issues	Japan	UK	France	Ireland	Germany	Sweden	Spain	Austria
					Significant difference (chi square)			
Trust	**	**	**			**		
Quality of dialogue	**	**	**			**		**
Understanding	**	**	**			**		**
Implementation	**	**	**		**	**		**
Strategically oriented	**	**			**			**
Individual performance		**		**				**
Tolerance	**	**		**		**	**	**

Note: ** Significant at the 01 level

pursuit of existing guidelines. In contrast, Irish and Spanish top management teams consider that inconsistency of decision implementation exists at senior management levels, in that should difficult or sensitive decisions need to be actioned, many senior managers tend to implement only those decisions that personally suit the individual.

In terms of strategic orientation, Japanese, British, German and Austrian top managers are identified as addressing both short- and long-term issues, according to the requirements of the company. In fact, the feeling portrayed is that management should be flexible in terms of responding to external pressures and needs. Certain managers found it difficult to state which objectives are more short or long term largely because of their willingness to be responsive to external conditions. However, French, Irish, Swedish and Spanish senior managers, due to the pressures in their company and the dynamics in the senior management committees, highlight that managing the organization is more geared to addressing short-term issues.

Despite the strategic orientation of the Germans and the levels of trust and quality of dialogue exhibited by the French, the respondents from France and Germany consider that greater tolerance of each other is required by the senior managers of their own colleagues. The reason given is that the task orientation of the Germans and the combative nature of debate amongst the French can undermine the nurture of good-quality colleague relationships. At an individual level, the British, Irish and Austrians feel that the performance of particular individual members of the top team requires attention, an issue that has remained unaddressed.

Issues requiring attention

Japanese, Irish, German, Spanish and Austrian senior managers report a substantial diversity of views existing at top management levels concerning future direction and strategy (Table 5.9). For the Japanese, issues of control of costs and quality are viewed as problematic. An issue for the British that is high on the agenda is cost management and control. For the Japanese, the challenge of appropriately responding to market needs is seen as requiring attention. Approaches to sales and marketing, understanding of competitor behaviour and servicing commitments to clients are identified as areas needing improvement. Equally, British, French and Austrian senior managers share concerns of sales and marketing, whereas the French feel that understanding competitors and their intentions is a concern. In addition to the Japanese, British and Irish senior managers feel that attention needs to be given to meeting client commitments, with the Irish in particular displaying the greatest level of concern for poor customer focus and, together with the Austrians, for overall quality of service delivery.

Table 5.9 Issues requiring attention (manufacturing)

Issues	Significant difference (chi square)							
	Japan	UK	France	Ireland	Germany	Sweden	Spain	Austria
Diversity of vision	**			**	**		**	**
Structure			**	**		**		**
Costs	**	**		**	**		**	
Quality	**			**	**		**	
Morale	**			**	**		**	**
Future of company	**	**		**	**		**	**
Customer focus				**				
Sales/marketing	**	**	**					**
Competitor analysis	**		**					
Trust	**		**	**				**
Departmental relations			**	**				**
Commitment to bosses			**					**
Commitment to clients	**	**		**				
Service delivery				**				**
Employee performance	**		**	**			**	**

Note: ** Significant at the 01 level

In terms of formal and more structured internal organizational relationships the French, Irish and Austrians indicate that departmental relations require attention and, for the French and Austrians in particular, meeting commitments to superiors requires improvement. People performance issues are equally seen as areas requiring improvement. Japanese, Irish, German, Spanish and Austrian senior managers regard maintenance of morale as a prime area of attention. In addition, maintaining high levels of employee performance, especially under circumstances of organizational change, is seen as a priority for attention by Japanese, French, Irish, Spanish and Austrian senior managers. Further, enhancing existing levels of trust between staff and management is seen as important by Japanese, French, Irish and Austrian managers. Overall, Japanese, Irish, French and Austrian senior managers consider issues of strategy, operational management, client responsiveness and employee development as key areas for improvement in organizational performance.

RETAIL SECTOR: RESULTS

Eight key areas of significant difference between these eight countries are identified, namely demographics, satisfaction with work, attitudes towards specialization of work, attitudes towards control/independence, attitudes to the company, effectiveness/ineffectiveness of follow through, differences of style of management and issues that are considered to require attention within the organization.

Demographics

Age of senior managers and the number of years spent in the company are identified as significantly different. The survey highlights that Japan has a greater proportion of managers in senior-level positions over the age of 55 (Table 5.10). In contrast, Britain, Ireland, Germany and Sweden highlight a greater proportion of top managers under the age of 46. Equally, Japanese senior managers report that they have remained in the company significantly longer than the remaining senior managers in the sample. The greater proportion of Japanese senior managers have remained employed in the same company for over twenty years, whereas French and Austrian senior managers report that a significant proportion of their sample have been in the company for under four years.

Work satisfaction

Higher levels of job satisfaction are reported by the senior managers of Japan, Britain, Ireland, Sweden and Austria (Table 5.11). However, the

Table 5.10 Demographics (retail)

Issues	Japan	UK	France	Ireland	Germany	Sweden	Spain	Austria
					Significant difference (chi square)			
Age	>55	<46		<46	<46	<46		
Company years	>20		<4					<4

Table 5.11 Work satisfaction (retail)

Issue	Japan	UK	France	Ireland	Germany	Sweden	Spain	Austria
					Significant difference (chi square)			
Job satisfaction	**	**		**		**		**
Growth opportunities	**	**				**		
Communicating contribution	**	**				**	**	
Colleague understanding	**	**		**	**	**	**	**
Clarity of responsibilities	**	**		**	**	**	**	**
Commitment	**	**	**	**		**	**	
Over-sensitive		**	**	**		**	**	**
Stress			**			**		

Note: ** Significant at the 01 level

opportunities for further growth in the job are identified by only Japanese, British and Swedish senior managers. In terms of helping colleagues and subordinates understand the nature of one's own job and the contribution required to promote high levels of performance, the Japanese, British, Swedish and Spanish managers report that they are more likely to make the effort at such communication. Only the French report a lack of clarity concerning key areas of responsibility in senior manager jobs. Again, only the French report lower levels of subordinate and colleague understanding of the job of senior managers in the organization. The French, together with the Swedish senior managers, report higher levels of stress experienced in the job. Despite the concerns reported by the French, their commitment to the job, as that of the Japanese, British, Irish, Swedish and Spanish, is reported as high. The British, French, Irish, Swedish, Spanish and Austrian senior managers report that they are over-sensitive to criticism concerning their performance as senior managers.

Specialist orientation

British, French and Irish senior managers report that the greatest degree of satisfaction comes from the specialist/technical aspects of their job (Table 5.12). However, only the French report that they feel more comfortable interacting with others from a similar technical background. The British, French, Spanish and Austrian senior managers report that they like to be considered as experts in their job. Further, the British, German, Spanish and Austrian senior managers report they value being members of a profession. Japanese senior managers do not identify specialization as a significant influence in terms of job-related performance.

Independence orientation

The need for self-determination is displayed strongest amongst British and Irish managers (Table 5.13). They report that they prefer to determine work patterns and schedules as they see fit. However, the French, Germans and Austrians report resentment towards being controlled. In terms of needing to be seen in control in order to do their job, the British, French, Germans and Austrians display a higher level of need.

All but the Swedish and Spanish report that they dislike the interference they experience in their job, whilst all but the Irish report that getting their own way as a senior manager is an important concern.

Attitudes to the company

The Japanese, British, French and Irish senior managers consider that the traditions of the organization should be respected (Table 5.14). The

Table 5.12 Specialist orientation (retail)

Issue	Japan	UK	France	Ireland	Germany	Sweden	Spain	Austria
			Significant difference (chi square)					
Satisfaction		**	**	**				
Ease of communication			**					
Considered expert		**	**				**	**
Professional membership		**			**		**	**

Note: ** Significant at the 01 level

Table 5.13 Independence orientation (retail)

Issue	Japan	UK	France	Ireland	Germany	Sweden	Spain	Austria
			Significant difference (chi square)					
Self-determination		**		**				
Resentment of control			**		**			**
Dislike interference	**	**	**	**	**			**
Need for control		**	**		**		**	**
Get own way	**	**	**		**	**	**	**

Note: ** Significant at the 01 level

Table 5.14 Attitudes to the company (retail)

Issues	Japan	UK	France	Ireland	Germany	Sweden	Spain	Austria
			Significant difference (chi square)					
Traditions	**	**	**	**				
Profit commitment		**	**	**	**		**	**
Change		**	**	**		**		**

Note: ** Significant at the 01 level

Japanese and Swedish report lower levels of positive response to commitment to pursuing profit. Japanese senior managers and to a lesser extent Swedish senior managers, feel that other factors need to be taken into account than having people in the organization totally committed to generating revenue.

Further, the Japanese, German and Spanish senior managers are less favourable in their comments towards the changes that have taken place in their organization. German and Spanish senior managers in particular feel that their company has been misguided with certain of the changes that have been undertaken. Japanese senior managers, although not as critical, highlight greater uncertainty as to the positive benefit of the changes experienced in their company.

Follow through

Japanese, British, Swedish, Spanish and Austrian senior managers indicate that discipline is fundamental to the successful operation of the organization (Table 5.15). In fact, further analysis indicates that Japanese, French and Spanish managers feel that the staff and management in their organization need to exhibit greater discipline than currently is the case.

Part of operating in a disciplined manner is to establish clear parameters and a well-structured way of operating, a view shared by Japanese, French, British, German, Spanish and Austrian senior managers. For the French and Germans establishing clear parameters is sufficient. They do not exhibit as strong a concern over being disciplined as managers. Ironically, French and German senior managers acknowledge that their staff and management need to exhibit greater application on following through on new initiatives. French senior managers, in particular, highlight that the managers in their organization lose track of developments on new and established initiatives.

In addition, British, French, Swedish and Spanish senior managers indicate that they promote clear procedures to enhance the management of the organization. Further, British, French, German and Austrian senior managers' opinion is that their staff and management are more rule bound, questioning less the direction they have been given. However, respect for protocol is exhibited more by Japanese and German managers. All of the senior managers in the sample indicate that they pay attention to receiving feedback and progress updates on current initiatives. As far as team work is concerned, Japanese, British, French and Spanish senior managers indicate that greater attention needs to be given to enhancing team cohesion in their organization.

Table 5.15 Follow-through (retail)

Issues	Japan	UK	France	Ireland	Germany	Sweden	Spain	Austria
					Significant difference (chi square)			
Discipline	**	**				**	**	**
Lose track			**					
Need more discipline			**		**			
Setting parameters	**	**	**		**		**	**
Clear procedures		**	**			**	**	
Progress updates	**	**	**	**	**	**	**	**
Rule bound		**	**		**			**
Protocol	**				**			
Team cohesion	**	**	**				**	

Note: ** Significant at the 01 level

Management style

All but the French and the British consider that they are seen by subordinates and colleagues as mature and tolerant individuals (Table 5.16). The French, together with the Spanish senior managers, indicate that they are seen as displaying their feelings either positively or negatively and can be considerably emotional in their response to other people or comments. The French and Germans are the only two groups in the sample who consider that improvements are required in the way meetings are managed and improvements in the styles displayed by their managers during meetings. Running meetings effectively is viewed as a particular concern by the managers of these two nationalities.

Issues requiring attention

Japanese, German and Spanish senior managers report the greatest number of concerns requiring attention (Table 5.17). Japanese senior managers indicate that the quality of internal relationships, the morale and performance of staff, responding effectively to market needs, being customer focused, and current sales and marketing practices, are in need of improvement within the organization. Further, the Japanese consider that greater attention needs to be given to issues of quality and control of costs. In fact, the results indicate that unless these issues are addressed, the respondents feel that the future of their company is under threat.

German and Spanish senior managers highlight similar challenges. For the German and Spanish respondents issues of organization structure, not being able to meet internal commitments, the current portfolio of services, quality and control of costs issues are identified as requiring attention.

The French and Irish report that improvements in organization structure, customer focus and staff performance are required, with the Irish, in particular, highlighting trust amongst colleagues and supervisors/subordinates as an additional sensitivity. For the Austrians, staff performance, current approaches to sales and marketing not adequately meeting internal (to the organization) commitments, and quality and cost control matters are the key issues that need examination.

SERVICES SECTOR: RESULTS

Nine areas of significant difference have emerged, namely, issues of demography, work satisfaction, orientation towards being specialist, independence orientation, attitudes towards the company, effectiveness of follow through, management style, top team dynamics and areas requiring attention within the company.

Table 5.16 Management style (retail)

Issues	Japan	UK	France	Ireland	Germany	Sweden	Spain	Austria
				Significant difference (chi square)				
Emotionality			**				**	
Meetings style			**		**			
Maturity	**			**	**	**	**	**
Criticism			**					
Uncommunicative		**						

Note: ** Significant at the 01 level

Table 5.17 Issues requiring attention (retail)

Issues	Japan	UK	France	Ireland	Germany	Sweden	Spain	Austria
					Significant difference (chi square)			
Structure			**	**	**		**	
Customer focus	**		**	**	**		**	
Staff morale	**				**		**	
Trust	**			**	**		**	
Internal commitments					**		**	**
Company future	**				**		**	
Sales/marketing	**				**		**	**
Staff performance	**		**	**	**		**	**
Response to market	**				**		**	
Services delivery	**				**		**	
Quality	**				**		**	**
Control of costs	**				**		**	**

Note: ** Significant at the 01 level

Demographics

A greater proportion of Japanese senior managers are identified as over 55 years old than their European counterparts in comparable positions (Table 5.18). Irish and German senior managers are identified as having a significantly greater number under the age of 46 years than the other country respondents.

A significantly greater level of Japanese and Irish senior managers have occupied their position for under one year, whereas British and Austrian senior managers in comparable positions have been in the same job for over ten years. In terms of years spent in the same company, a greater number of Japanese, Irish, German and Swedish senior mangers have spent more than twenty years in the same company, whereas a significantly greater number of French and Spanish senior managers have spent less than four years in their present organization. In terms of clarity of communication of functional objectives, the French and Spanish senior managers highlight less effective practice in this area than the other respondents. In addition, French, Irish and Spanish senior managers highlight poorer quality of communication of comporate objectives, than the other respondents in the sample.

Work satisfaction

All respondents except for the French senior managers report significantly high levels of job satisfaction (Table 5.19). Equally, all respondents except for the French senior managers report significantly high levels of opportunities for growth in their jobs. In terms of managing stress, Japanese, British, Irish, Spanish and Austrian senior managers report a greater level of capability in this area than the remaining respondents. Additional information gleaned from the study, although not reported in Table 5.17, highlights that German and Swedish managers indicate that they feel themselves vulnerable to sustained pressure of work. Further, French senior managers emphasize that they are particularly prone to the stresses of work.

All but Japanese senior managers report that they can be over-sensitive to criticism and to the opinions that others hold of them. However, Japanese, British, German, Swedish, Spanish and Austrian senior managers indicate that their colleagues are understanding of the issues and pressures they face in their role. The reason is that these individuals report that they have made an effort to talk to colleagues about the demands they face in their role and the means they have used to address such demands. Overall, French and German senior managers highlight greater levels of dissatisfaction in that they wish to leave their present jobs.

Table 5.18 Services sector

Issues	Japan	UK	France	Ireland	Germany	Sweden	Spain	Austria
					Significant difference (chi square)			
Age	>55			<46	<46			
Job years	<1	>10		<1				>10
Company years	>20		<4	>20	>20	>20	<4	
Functional objectives	**	**		**	**	**		**
Corporate objectives	**	**			**	**		**

Note: ** Significant at the 01 level

Table 5.19 Work satisfaction (services)

Issues	Japan	UK	France	Ireland	Germany	Sweden	Spain	Austria
				Significant difference (chi square)				
Job satisfaction	**	**		**	**	**	**	**
Stress management	**	**		**			**	**
Colleague understanding	**	**			**	**	**	**
Growth opportunities	**	**		**	**	**	**	**
Over-sensitive		**	**	**	**	**	**	**
Leave job			**		**			

Note: ** Significant at the 01 level

Specialist orientation

French, German and Austrian senior managers report that their greatest satisfaction at work comes from the technical/specialist part of their job (Table 5.20). Further, especially the French, along with Spanish senior managers, indicate that they find it easier to communicate with staff and managers from a similar technical background. In terms of personal satisfaction, British, French and German senior managers highlight that they enjoy the specialist aspects of their job more than the general management aspects.

Other than the Japanese and Swedish senior managers, the remaining respondents consider that they like to be seen as experts. In addition, British, Irish, German, Spanish and Austrian senior managers state that they value being a member of a profession. Japanese senior managers highlight no significant response to a work-related specialism.

Independence orientation

British, French, Irish and Swedish report that they like being in a position where others do not have control over them (Table 5.21). Further, in terms of day-to-day tasks and activities, British and Irish senior managers display a need for determining how their subordinates' work should be allocated and managed. Equally, British, French and Austrian senior managers state that they are motivated by being in a position of control.

Although British and Irish senior managers are more likely to display a greater need for independence, they indicate that they are unlikely to respond negatively should control measures be applied to them. However, French, German and Austrian senior managers report that they are more likely to resent and display their resentment at attempts to control. Whatever feelings are expressed towards control and self-determination, all but Swedish senior managers report that they dislike the experience of interference in their work or in the making and implementing of decisions. Overall, the Swedes report least negative reaction to control.

Attitudes to company

Japanese, French, German, Swedish and Austrian senior managers report satisfaction with the quality and effectiveness of the financial controls in their company (Table 5.22). In contrast, British, Irish and Spanish senior managers specifically highlight that money is wasted in their company because of ineffective financial controls. A positive attitude to the current systems and controls is expressed by the Japanese, British, French, Swedish and Spanish senior managers. Counteracting

Table 5.20 Specialist orientation (services)

Issues	Significant difference (chi square)							
	Japan	UK	France	Ireland	Germany	Sweden	Spain	Austria
Specialist satisfaction			**		**			**
Technical communication			**				**	
Expertise		**	**	**	**		**	**
Professional membership		**		**	**		**	**
Specialist preference		**	**		**			

Note: ** Significant at the 01 level

Table 5.21 Independence orientation (services)

Issues	Significant difference (chi square)							
	Japan	UK	France	Ireland	Germany	Sweden	Spain	Austria
Self-determination		**	**	**		**		
Work determination		**		**				
Control resentment			**		**			**
Dislike interference	**	**	**	**	**		**	**
Being boss		**	**					**

Note: ** Significant at the 01 level

Table 5.22 Attitudes towards the company (services)

Issues	Significant difference (chi square)							
	Japan	UK	France	Ireland	Germany	Sweden	Spain	Austria
Financial controls	**		**		**	**		**
Job stability	**	**	**	**		**	**	**
Tradition	**	**	**	**				
Systems and controls	**	**	**			**	**	
Change (positive)		**		**		**		
Change (negative)		**	**	**			**	

Note: ** Significant at the 01 level

such a perspective, Irish, German and Austrian senior managers consider that the current systems and controls in their company are a hindrance to the completion of tasks and the pursuit of initiatives. Further, the Germans are the only respondents who feel that their managers do not experience job stability. In fact, certain German companies report that their managers are relocated at an alarmingly increasing rate.

From a more general perspective, Japanese, British, French and Irish senior managers indicate that they respect the traditions of their company. As far as change is concerned, British, Irish and Swedish senior managers feel that most of the changes in their company have been introduced for good reason. Further, over the longer term, these changes are identified as having produced positive results.

However, where change is identified as having gone wrong, greatest criticism is expressed by British, French, Irish and Spanish senior managers. They report that their company was misguided to pursue certain of the changes they undertook. The British and Irish respondents provide the greatest contrast of view concerning the management of change. Both suggest that their experience of change in the services sector has been experienced as both positive and negative. Such experiences are driven by circumstances unique to particular organizations rather than common across the services sector.

Follow through

Japanese, British, Irish, German, Swedish, Spanish and Austrian senior managers consider behaving in a disciplined way to be fundamental to achieving success for the organization (Table 5.23). Also specifically highlighted by the same senior managers is the need for discipline in meetings in terms of making contributions, listening to others, sticking to the agenda and timetable, in order to satisfactorily fulfil the agenda. The French do not rate discipline as highly as the other senior managers in the sample. However, the French together with the Japanese, British, Irish, German and Austrian senior managers state that senior management, overall, needs to be more disciplined at follow through. Japanese, British and French senior managers consider that setting parameters for how work should be conducted assists the process of follow through and the pursuing of objectives. However, only the British, French, Swedish and Spanish senior managers feel that it is important to follow established work procedures.

French and German senior managers, but also to an extent Spanish and Austrian senior managers, consider that abiding by established rules and procedures is a necessary way to achieve effective follow through. In addition, Japanese, Swedish and Austrian senior managers consider that paying attention to protocol is important in conveying an

Table 5.23 Follow through (services)

Issues	Japan	UK	France	Ireland	Germany	Sweden	Spain	Austria
					Significant difference (chi square)			
Discipline	**	**		**	**	**	**	**
Work parameters	**	**	**					
Procedures		**	**			**	**	
Rule bound			**		**		**	**
Protocol	**					**		**
Lose track			**	**				
Team cohesion	**	**	**	**			**	
Briefings	**	**	**	**	**	**	**	**

Note: ** Significant at the 01 level

image of a disciplined management. In contrast, British, French, Irish, German and Spanish senior managers indicate that they are more likely to act in a way that seems appropriate for the circumstances and observe the protocol later. Further, maintaining team cohesion is considered by Japanese, British, French, Irish and Spanish senior managers as a necessary element of follow through.

French and Irish senior managers highlight that because of their style and the pressures facing them and the demands made on their organization, losing track of projects and initiatives occurs with regularity. However, whatever the styles and challenges identified by the different groups of respondents, briefings are highly valued as a fundamental element of follow through. All respondents state that they insist on being regularly briefed, especially concerning new initiatives.

Management style

French and Austrian senior managers highlight that their subordinates and colleagues consider them as being too emotional in their behaviour and in their response to challenges, in terms of reacting to circumstances and events rather than objectively thinking through appropriate ways of behaving (Table 5.24). However, only the French senior managers indicate that they respond adversely to critical comment. In contrast, British, Irish, German, Spanish and Austrian senior managers consider themselves more uncommunicative by indicating that it takes time for other people to get to know them.

All, except the Japanese respondents, consider themselves as more mature in their outlook and managerial style and feel that is how their colleagues view them. Other than the Japanese and Swedish senior managers, the other respondents highlight that the focus of their style is to motivate staff and management to make the organization more profitable. Further, other than the Spanish senior managers, all of the other respondents indicate that developing a style that assists them and their subordinates to better nurture customer relationships, is an important issue in managing people.

Top team

Japanese, British, French, Swedish and Austrian senior managers identify quality of dialogue as an important ingredient to the effective functioning of senior management teams (Table 5.25). They indicate that they are more able, despite experiencing discomfort, to address and discuss sensitive issues than the Irish, German and Spanish senior managers in the sample. However, all indicate that they genuinely

Table 5.24 Management style (services)

Issues	Significant difference (chi square)							
	Japan	UK	France	Ireland	Germany	Sweden	Spain	Austria
Emotionality			**					**
Uncommunicative		**		**	**		**	**
Sensitivity	**						**	**
Maturity		**	**	**	**	**	**	**
Criticism			**					
Profitability		**	**	**	**		**	**
Customer	**	**	**	**	**	**		**

Note: ** Significant at the 01 level

Table 5.25 Top team (services)

Issues	Significant difference (chi square)							
	Japan	UK	France	Ireland	Germany	Sweden	Spain	Austria
Quality dialogue	**	**	**			**		**
Implementation	**	**	**	**	**	**	**	**
Tolerance	**	**				**	**	**
Inhibition				**			**	
Trust	**	**				**	**	**

Note: ** Significant at the 01 level

attempt to implement decisions that have jointly been made rather than implement those decisions that personally suit the individual.

Japanese, British, Swedish, Spanish and Austrian senior managers highlight that, as colleagues, they are more understanding of each other as people. Equally, Japanese, British, Swedish and Austrian senior managers indicate that they are more understanding than the remaining respondents of the pressures faced by their colleagues. Interestingly, Irish and Spanish senior managers highlight greater levels of inhibition in terms of bringing to the surface sensitivities that require attention. Equally, they indicate that they are less likely to confront each other as colleagues to discuss shared concerns. Moreover, Japanese, British, Swedish, Spanish and Austrian senior managers rate themselves as more trustworthy and consider themselves as more trusted by their colleagues and subordinates, than French, Irish and German senior managers.

Issues requiring attention

Japanese, Irish and Austrian senior managers identify the greatest number of concerns requiring attention (Table 5.26). Six issues regarding performance in the market are identified. Japanese, Irish and Austrian senior managers consider that improvements are required in sales and marketing, in responding to customer needs, in responding appropriately to initiatives being promoted by competitors (only Japanese and Irish) in better meeting commitments to clients (only Japanese) and in meeting deadlines and delivering on time (Irish and Austrian). Further, for Japanese, Irish and Austrian senior managers, the portfolio of services offered by their organization is considered as inadequate and in need of re-examination. All others identify concerns internal to the organization as requiring attention, except for the Swedish respondents, who identify that comparatively no significant issues need attention. Finally, improvements in quality are more identified as concerns by Japanese and Spanish senior managers.

Referring to organizational related issues, increasing levels of cost are viewed as problematic by Japanese, British, Irish, Spanish and Austrian senior managers. Improvements in and changes to organization structure are identified only by Japanese senior managers, as worthy of attention. The quality of interdepartmental and functional relations is considered by French, Irish, Spanish and Austrian senior managers as needing improvement.

However, in the area of people-related matters, most of the respondents identify certain issues needing attention. Improving levels of trust between senior managers and between senior management and the remaining employees in the organization are seen by all of the respondents, except

Table 5.26 Issues requiring attention (services)

Issues	Japan	UK	France	Ireland	Germany	Sweden	Spain	Austria
						Significant difference (chi square)		
Costs	**	**		**			**	**
Quality	**						**	**
Sales/marketing	**			**				**
Customers	**			**				**
Competitors	**			**				
Internal relations			**	**			**	**
Structure	**							
Initiatives	**			**				**
Commitments to bosses								**
Commitments to clients	**							
Service delivery				**				**
Employee performance	**		**	**			**	**
Trust	**	**	**	**	**		**	**
Morale	**		**	**	**		**	**

Note: ** Significant at the 01 level

the Swedish senior managers, as an issue which requires continuous attention. Morale in the organization is seen by all except for the British and Swedish senior managers as requiring improvement. Further, the overall performance of employees is viewed more by Japanese, French, Irish, Spanish and Austrian senior managers as problematic than the remaining respondents. However, in terms of meeting commitments to supervisors, only Austrian senior managers see this concern as worthy of improvement.

SUMMARY

Japan/Europe: across the three sectors

- Japanese senior managers are identified as older than their European counterparts.
- Japanese managers are identified as being employed longer in the same company than their European counterparts in manufacturing and retail, but comparable with Irish, German and Swedish managers in the services sector.
- Japanese senior managers display higher levels of work satisfaction than their European counterparts across the three sectors.
- Japanese senior managers display a greater sensitivity and more positive attitude to addressing challenges of a general management nature than their European counterparts across the three sectors. It is worth noting the contradiction of this finding with the findings in Chapter 3 over inabilities to address sensitive concerns and the tensions between the policy makers and implementors on the one hand and business drivers on the other. Whether the greater inclination of the Japanese towards general management survives is questionable.
- Only in the manufacturing sector are corporate/functional objectives identified as more effectively communicated by the Japanese than by the other European respondents.
- Japanese and Swedish senior managers display lower need for control than the other European respondents across the three sectors.
- Displaying a positive attitude towards the organization is identified as varying more by sector than by nationality. Only in the services sector are Japanese senior managers identified as displaying a more positive attitude towards their company than the other senior European managers in the sample.
- Effective follow through in terms of personal and team discipline, team cohesion, respect for protocol, positive communication through effectively conducted briefings and establishing clear parameters within which staff and management have the discretion to respond

to external changes, is identified as varying more by sector than by nationality.

- Attitudes towards change are identified as varying more by sector than by nationality.
- Sensitivity of managerial style in order to enhance relationships with customers, supervisors, colleagues and subordinates are identified as varying more by sector than by nationality.
- Quality of dialogue and trust between senior managers is identified as varying more by sector than by nationality.
- Senior managers responding maturely to critical comment and being sensitive to feedback are identified as varying more by sector than by nationality.
- Issues that are considered as requiring attention, such as issues of customer and marketplace performance, costs, product/service quality, product/services portfolio, formal organizational relationships, staff performance and morale and the future of the company, are identified as varying more by sector than by nationality, although the Japanese respondents, irrespective of sector, consistently highlight most of these concerns as needing attention more than their European counterparts.

Part III
Implications for management development

'Paradoxical' is one word that summarizes the nature of the results of the Japanese top manager survey.

On the one hand, the approaches of seeking consensus, attaining effectiveness of communication and promoting a satisfactory work environment, are identified as positive and enhancing. On the other, the disciplined, follow through, results-oriented style counterbalances the 'softer' approaches, but significantly correlates with promoting disruptive and inhibitingly tense working relationships. Equally, the Japanese respondents emerge as the most cohesive in terms of identifying with the mission of their organization (98 per cent), as portraying higher levels of trust and consistency of behaviour, and as more satisfied with their job and work in comparison to the managers from other European countries. In contrast, however, the Japanese respondents highlight the greatest degree of difficulty in addressing known concerns, when compared to the European respondents which is especially the case when contrasting the different issues highlighted across the three sectors of manufacturing, retail and services. Across these three sectors the Japanese highlight the greatest number of concerns requiring attention. In effect, the Japanese respondents indicate that they can trust each other and jointly move forward, sharing a sense of collective responsibility more than the Europeans, and yet find it considerably difficult to address those issues that need attention in order to promote an added-value service. Furthermore, certain other leadership levers such as discipline in meetings, consistency of follow through and sensitivity of managerial style are identified as varying by sector, rather than by nationality in terms of effectiveness of practice when compared to the Europeans. Hence, in terms of leadership effectiveness, the Japanese seem no better or more able than anyone else. What is the impact of such a paradox in providing for effective leadership under circumstances of conflicting stakeholder demands being made on the organization?

In the foyer of the London office of the Fujitsû subsidiary ICL, a notice clearly reads, 'Do 1000 Things, 1% Better'. This interesting phrase encapsulates the essence of the 'stakeholder value organization', namely, the organization and its infrastructure are well constituted and focused, but sustained competitive advantage comes from constant attention to all those little things that together make the difference. Under these circumstances, making the difference is not something that can be prescribed, but more a requirement of effective leadership responsive to the demands of each context.

Chapter 6

Developing leaders

The top must be innovating. Your function is to stimulate your staff and also management level to be as innovative as you, and try to get younger people to have some opportunity.
(Chief Executive Officer, financial services company in Japan)

KEY ISSUES

Confronting internal to the organization and sensitive people issues is a key concern for Japanese business leaders. It is recognized that the productivity of white-collar workers and the rapidly changing values of younger people are having a severe impact on Japanese business organizations. It is also similarly recognized that if the quality of internal dialogue were to improve, there would equally be improvements in operational, strategic and people performance. Hence, in terms of developing leaders, attention is given to focusing on those questions, that if addressed, could enhance on-the-job performance as well as identifying key management development levers for the training of current managers and those entering into middle and senior positions.

Acknowledging reality

Paying attention to those concerns that require discussion, especially when discussion is difficult, is identified as crucial in today's world. The leadership that can knit together conflicting demands, is the leadership required for an organization that can effectively respond to conflicting stakeholder demands. In order to promote such effectiveness, it is necessary to recognize the reality of what is happening in Japanese business organizations in order to effectively promote the development of leaders. Hence, in the following discussion, attention is given to acknowledging the reality within Japanese organization as a prelude to then examining improvements in dialogue, ways of promoting how to enhance expatriate placement and general management development.

What issues do the Japanese respondents find difficult to raise? The most highly quoted areas of sensitivity for dialogue are outlined as follows:

	No.	%
• Productivity of white-collar workers	265	35
• Issues affecting long term	205	27
• Leadership style	184	24
• Decline of young people	180	24
• Different values held by young people	170	22
• Cost management and control	168	22
• Relationship between departments	164	22
• Future of the company	162	21

Supporting the questionnaire results, the interviews with the top Japanese managers highlight the ever-growing concern over white-collar productivity. The only significant and consistent theme about white-collar productivity to emerge is the seeming lack of insight as to how to manage this problem.

Other than that, the above remaining issues can be classified into two groupings: relationship-oriented and being strategic. As can be seen, the relationship-oriented issues are highlighted with greater frequency than the strategy issues. Top Japanese managers are finding the people-related issues as the more difficult to address. Interestingly, leadership style has emerged as the most dominant of the people-oriented issues that needs attention.

In effect, the manner in which Japanese companies function is the concern. Further, comparisons of the three sectors of manufacturing, retail/wholesale and services highlight that the Japanese are fundamentally no better prepared to confront business and organizational change than the Europeans. In fact, in the retail sector, 82 per cent of the Japanese respondents felt that issues considered as sensitive, but merited attention, remained unaddressed in senior management circles. Eighty-one per cent of Spanish and 75 per cent of Austrian respondents in the retail sector also identify considerable inhibitions in addressing known and sensitive challenges in their own organizations.

Whatever else is done, the first major step is to acknowledge the nature of challenges that exist and promote concern at senior levels of management. Certain writers consider that the response of Japanese management to address people and strategy problems has been piece-meal (Ito 1993b). However, some companies have recognized that restructuring also requires reconsideration of boardroom membership and patterns of communication (Watanabe and Yamamoto 1992). The Shin Nittetsu employee reduction has been accompanied by a reduction of four board directors to a total of forty-four (Shigeta and Morita 1994). In contrast, the NTT restructuring of personnel progressed against a background where there had been over the previous ten years an increase of board directors from twenty-two to thirty-six (Shigeta and Morita 1994). The new Mitsubishi Chemicals, a creation from the merger between Mitsubishi Kasei and Mitsubishi Petrochemicals, has fifty directors, a reduction of twelve from the sum of directors of the two original companies. Moreover, accompanying the merger is a structure of subsidiary companies to replace the previous business divisions, emphasizing the financial independence of the different companies. In order to emphasize the philosophy of decentralization, each of the executive directors has been placed as the CEO of those subsidiaries, thereby strengthening the responsibility of the board directors. Professor Itami of Hitotsubashi University remarks that 'merger offers the best opportunity for reduction of the size of the board. It may hurt a bit at the time, but is like dealing with the medical problem by the use of laser therapy' (Shigeta and Morita 1994).

The situation at the Sakura Bank is a case in point. At the time of the merger between the Mitsui Bank and Taiyo-Kobe Bank, the directors of both banks were transferred to the board of the new bank, creating a mammoth board of sixty-six people. It took the bank four years to reduce it to fifty-nine (Shigeta and Morita 1994).

Three vice-presidents of Toho Life Insurance resigned in June 1994, taking responsibility for the loss at the end of the 1993 financial year. As for its president, Ota, another term of office was ensured because of his 'charisma' or 'centripetal effect' on employee loyalty, thus renewing his record of tenure as president for seventeen years (Shigeta and Morita 1994).

At Japan Victor, five *torishimariyaku* (directors) including the chairman and the four senior managing directors resigned in 1992. It was part of the 'rejuvenation strategy' implemented by its president who at the age of 56 was in his second term of office and wanted a younger board (Shigeta and Morita 1994).

Despite examples of boardroom restructuring, reform at senior management levels has been slow to take off. Further, in terms of holding individual directors more accountable for company results, the issue of effective leadership of Japanese organizations still remains poorly addressed.

Enhancement of dialogue

Having identified key areas of sensitivity, the Japanese respondents were asked to list how much better would things be if such concerns had been resolved earlier. The list below outlines the most quoted issues:

	No.	%
• Improved employee morale	323	42
• Increased profitability	299	39
• Improved clarity of strategic direction	268	35
• Better employee performance	262	34
• Improved response to new initiatives	257	34
• Improved quality of decision making	228	30
• Greater trust	195	26
• Greater commitment to decisions	190	25
• Fewer inaccuracies to clients/customers	158	21
• Better focus on customer groups	154	20

Other than the issue of increased profitability, the remaining areas of improvement represent people-driven challenges. It is postulated that attention to the 'softer' synergies provides the extra cutting edge in terms of customer loyalty, customer retention, effectively determining longer-term relationships and effective marketing. This is likely to especially be the case for Japanese business organizations as the questionnaire highlighted the following interesting views.

The following questions were asked:

Q: How would you rate your competitors?
A: Customer-oriented (61 per cent of responses)

Q: What is involved in the marketing of your products/services?
A: Establishing longer-term relationships with clients/customers (90 per cent of responses)

The evidence emerging from the Cranfield survey suggests that the content of senior management dialogue should emphasize the 'softer' concerns of management. Consideration of the following questions may assist senior Japanese managers to explore avenues for improvement:

• What key concerns are known to exist in the organization and are consistently not discussed at senior management levels?
• For how long have particular concerns been recognized as pertinent to address?
• What is the nature of the sensitivity that inhibits appropriate dialogue from taking place?
• What forums do senior management attend in order to examine and understand the workings of the organization?
• At these forums, who establishes the agenda, and how representative are the issues on the agenda in terms of any underlying but inadequately examined concerns?

- How responsive are senior management to giving and receiving feedback?
- To what extent do senior management seriously request feedback?
- How remote are senior management from the reality of organizational life?
- What are the opportunity costs for the business of not entering into dialogue over these issues?

The response to these questions is likely to provide a view as to management's intent and capability to discuss the issues facing their organization. As management in the future are likely to experience ever greater levels of ambiguity in responding to the conflicting demands of different stakeholders, the honest views emerging from the above questions are likely to highlight senior management's level of robustness to provide for effective leadership.

Considerations for expatriate placement

The business management literature is awash with books and articles on expatriate managers, for example (Brewster 1989; Brewster *et al.* 1991; Bjorkman and Gernsten 1990) the preparation of expatriates for placement (Tung 1988); their compensation packages (Schuler and Dowling 1988); approaches to monitoring their performance (Hedland 1986) and considerations for repatriation (Hanill 1989; Edstrom and Galbraith 1977).

However, the Cranfield survey results captured in Table 3.5 highlight an additional interesting finding, namely the impact of the various styles of Japanese business leaders on local European management. Most positive results are gained through effective communication, providing clarity of direction and generating circumstances which help local management to feel satisfied with the organization. A consensus-oriented approach is viewed positively, but as having less impact than the above three. The styles which induce more negative orientation, are those concerned with a need to enhance results but with less attention being given to relationship management. What is the consequence of these styles for Japanese expatriate managers?

Intensive case study analysis conducted by the Cranfield team in Europe has identified that adopting a leadership style that is viewed as inappropriate by the local country management, can have a detrimental impact on sales and marketing, a concern highlighted by 43 per cent of Japanese survey respondents (Kakabadse *et al.* 1995). The Japanese respondents indicate that the sales and marketing practised across a number of regions is inadequate and requires restructuring.

Crucial to adjusting to local conditions is the appreciation of differences within each locality in terms of sales and marketing. The Cranfield survey in Europe highlights that companies within the same industry sector, pursuing similar customers with comparable products, may display quite different approaches to sales and marketing. Why? Because regional variation is an important factor. What sales and marketing means for the same product range in Greece is likely to be different in the French market. Misunderstandings can easily arise as to the conditions and requirements of different markets in any region, or between regions. The time taken by the expatriate manager to appreciate the business circumstances they face is dependent on their ability to integrate locally.

Being able to integrate depends on the quality of relationships the expatriate manager evolves with local management. Obviously, one way to damage relationships is to adopt styles of leadership that the locals find unwelcome. Another way is to have targets set from the centre which are considered as unattainable in the operating business, due to local market conditions. A newly appointed expatriate senior manager, who too readily buys into targets set from above and against the advice of local management, faces the prospect of losing credibility with the local team. Targeting out of step with local market circumstances leads to defensiveness on the part of local managers. For the expatriate manager, this may mean renegotiating targets set by the centre. A common experience in multinationals is that whatever targets are set, they are prone to renegotiation (Kakabadse and Myers 1995). Effectively managing the process of negotiation, on especially cost and revenue targets, between corporate centre and the subsidiary, takes time to learn.

Local managers can quickly recognize when the targets they are given are out of keeping with the reality of their business circumstances. Within a short while, local management can become demotivated. A demotivated local management will demotivate the staff which in turn will have a negative effect on the performance of the organization.

The learning point is that it is necessary to understand the nature of the circumstances a company faces in different parts of Europe, or any other region of the world, and then build the necessary network of relationships in order to do business. The Cranfield survey highlights that those Japanese leaders most prone to not growing the necessary positive relationships with local management are the more results-oriented business drivers. For those Japanese organizations that may be facing problems with the indigenous management, consideration of the following questions may provide clues as to ways forward:

- Do constraints exist at local management level, in one or more country sites, within the multinational organization?
- Do problems of business and organization result from such constraints not being addressed?

- Is a non-greenfield site subsidiary being treated as a greenfield site situation?
- Have the constraints been identified and discussed with local management?
- To what extent is there ownership at local management and expatriate/corporate centre management levels, to address such constraints?
- To what extent has a partnership philosophy between local management and expatriate/corporate centre management been adopted to overcome the problems identified?
- To what extent have all the key interfaces been consistently nurtured so as to improve relationships and quality of dialogue?
- To what extent is expatriate management really listening to local management and attempting to integrate with local circumstances?
- If all else has been done, is it necessary to remove people?

Case study analyses conducted by the Cranfield team in Britain highlight that those Japanese companies that are more likely to face problems with local country management are those in non-greenfield site locations. In such situations, Japanese management has to manage and change an existing culture and does not have the luxury of starting with a clean sheet!

General management development

In the acknowledging reality section, style of leadership emerged as a topic that the respondents find difficult to discuss – why? First, hierarchical distance can make senior management be seen as too remote to involve in dialogue. Second, the quality of conversation, even though consensus is achieved, may be perceived as inadequate and not sufficiently penetrating. Whatever the reasons, such a finding indicates a deeply felt concern.

In order to strengthen existing management, and the younger emerging managers, to better address the issues they face, it is recommended that management style should be viewed in conjunction with meeting the challenge of effectively performing as a general manager. Therefore, several areas of general management development are outlined.

Career planning

Numerous managers from the Cranfield European study outlined the advantages of having experienced working in more than one function in the same firm, rather than working in more than one firm but staying in the same function, before the age of 35 years. The learning gained by crossing organizational boundaries provides the basis for being capable of communicating effectively with colleagues in other functions, once in a senior role. This system of development by rotation has been well instituted in large Japanese corporations and allows the Japanese managers to evolve the effective networking, on which the successful functioning of many organizational processes depend (Okazaki-Ward 1993).

The development of a solid overview of their organization should be greatly helped by the early experience of cross-function working, and this is all the more important since the Japanese regard the ability of the senior managers to have a global view of their organization very highly, only second to leadership ability in the Cranfield survey. However, the system of developmental rotation has too often been based on the expediency of company needs and individual preferences tended to take second place. Given that the up-and-coming generation is likely to need a more meaningful job experience to be well motivated, the system may require to become part of a career development programme in which individual preferences for the future course of career development are regarded as an input of equal importance in the existing human resources management practices in the Japanese company.

Promoting leadership experience

An additional area of practical development for prospective leaders is in the area of personal leadership. The implication is that individuals need to be given the responsibility for managing people. Unless a manager is exposed to learning how to allocate work, chair meetings, motivate team members, discuss understandable differences of opinion and reach resolution, and above all be held accountable for the decisions that have been made, the individual may not move to high office with the confidence that is required for effective performance. Other Cranfield studies conducted in the USA and UK indicate that most of the respondents received their first leadership position before the age of 30 years (Margerison and Kakabadse 1984). In the Japanese corporate context, where the practice of slow-burn promotion is still the norm, an early selection of future business leaders for training and leadership experience is probably difficult, particularly as a survey has shown that seniority consciousness is regarded as the greatest obstacle to such a change being introduced (Japan Management Association 1994b). Selection at too early a stage could adversely affect the morale of the remaining employees, and at the personal level, cause the selected individual to suffer intensive ill-will from his peers (Okazaki-Ward 1993).

Consequently, few companies (3.3 per cent) currently have a policy of selection and training before the age of 30 (Japan Management Association 1994b). However, 28 per cent of the top management think that such a process should begin at and around the age of 30, and 81 per cent regard a future provision of specific career path to facilitate this as necessary (Japan Management Association 1994b). Of respondents in the Japan Management Association survey, 83 per cent highlight being posted to a core function in head office as the most effective way of developing leadership capabilities. An early appointment to a middle-management position is cited as the second most effective way of developing future business leaders (66 per cent) (Japan Management Association 1994b). However, as 73 per cent of firms in the survey felt they lack the number of people fully developed to assume business leader positions (Japan Management Association 1994b), it is clear that the existing practice is not working effectively. An earlier start in leadership experience within a fast-track promotion system may be one of the possible, if long-term, solutions. Clearly, such an action, which amounts to merit-based promotion rather than the traditional one based on seniority, entails adjustments to many of the existing personnel arrangements, not least of which is to devise an effective way of selection relying on more objective measures seen to be fair and reliable by the employees.

General management training

General management programmes can be a valuable lever in developing the potential of those who exhibit the aptitude for senior office. From experience, the following elements have been considered as valuable in general management programmes.

- *Issues-based teaching.* A strategic perspective should be taken in the presentation of the key subject areas of finance, marketing, information systems, manufacturing strategy, design, business strategy and human resources management. Most of the major American and European business schools are teaching, or are working towards teaching, integrated case studies.
- *International and research driven.* Insights concerning improvements in MNCs (multinational corporations) and different regions of the world should be standard on most general management programmes. A 'cutting edge' programme is one which is research driven, highlighting the latest trends and practices across key markets, providing information on latest techniques and promoting new perspectives on issues, such as managing change. Added value, in terms of management development for the future, will depend on research results of a cross-comparative nature.
- *Current issues and society.* In order to prepare managers to lead the stakeholder value organization of the future, broader social, ethical and legal perspectives need to be adopted in order to stimulate an understanding of the key relationships between society and business.

Esoteric sociological and political science contributions will not do! Pragmatic teaching is required on those aspects of society that are likely to influence the criteria for decision making at general management level. For managers who work in mid- to large-sized corporations, taking a broader societal perspective provides the tools for considering medium- to long-term strategic developments, and, in effect, makes issues such as business ethics and corporate responsibility realistic concerns rather than ephemeral subjects.

Network of contacts

Making contact with other programme participants during and after the programme is an important element in executive development programmes. The calibre of the programme participants, and their experiences, are important ingredients in the success of a programme, and learning from each other and forming mentorship relationships can make a lasting impact on each manager. It is appreciated that networking within Japanese organizations and between affiliated companies has been effectively applied to date. But the question is, with the emerging business challenges, and increasing internationalization of business, will this continue to the same degree of effectiveness? Companies and business education organizations need to sponsor opportunities for managers to come into contact with their counterparts in other business organizations in different industrial sectors and in non-business organizations, and indeed, in other countries, in order to widen their management horizons.

Personal development

Personal development is the foundation for an executive-development programme. A high-calibre programme should bring together quantitative learning inputs such as strategy, functional business skills, and economic and political trends, with more qualitative concerns such as the personality of the manager and how that affects his/her performance and decision-making capacity, the importance of management style, and how attitude can be a powerful enabler or inhibitor to individual and team performance. Personal counselling, the use of psychological and management-style tests, and even well-planned outdoor activities, are fruitful mechanisms for helping managers understand what they are like as a person, how they 'naturally' manage, and what further on-the-job development experiences they need to undergo in order to stimulate greater improvement. Once learning becomes an emotional experience, especially if the manager is receiving feedback on his capacity to shape an identity for the function or organization for which he/she is accountable, or on how differences of personality and style could severely inhibit discussion within teams, or dampen the enthusiasm of others, it is likely that an impact will be made on how that manager performs at work. Each participant internalizes learning and gives serious consideration to what he/she will do on return to work. Hence, considerable time needs to be structured into the programme for group and/or individual counselling and feedback.

Conclusion

The ever greater demands being made on Japanese management are evident. This is ever more apparent as, in the *White Paper on the Enterprise* published in January 1994 by *Keizai Doyukai* (Keizai Doyukai 1994a), Japanese companies are portrayed as standing at a crossroads where the future is not clear and at the same time as having to undergo substantial structural changes, described as the biggest discontinuity since the end of World War II. Never has strong leadership been more earnestly sought from corporate top management than it is now. That 81 per cent of the Japanese respondents of the Cranfield Executive Competencies Survey cite leadership as the requirement for top management to effectively carry out its responsibility, placing it as the number one priority, is not surprising. Meeting the expectation of different stakeholders who impact on a business organization is a process fraught with ambiguity. Normality is likely to be a feeling of 'can we ever get it right?' The quality of leadership to provide a pathway through such ambiguous circumstances is a crucial factor in determining the effective performance of Japanese organizations.

In terms of qualities of leadership, the Cranfield survey highlights three crucial questions for Japanese managers to consider:

- To what extent does quality of dialogue (or the lack of it) among the members of the top team impact on the effectiveness of Japanese management?
- What are the management development issues facing Japanese managers in the future, bearing in mind that value differences between the more accepted approaches to management and the new ones emerging, for example, between policy makers and business drivers, in terms of ways of working and managing relationships, are likely to impact on the styles adopted in Japanese business organizations?
- What is the impact of the emerging Japanese management styles on local managers in overseas operations? Does further consideration need to be given to expatriate placement and length of expatriate tenure?

If nothing else, bearing in mind that the younger generation are increasingly less likely to accept certain current values, such as seniority-based promotion, and are equally likely to press for greater financial reward based on performance and merit, leadership for stakeholder value is likely to be a requirement for the future. Responding to the above three questions is a must, not an option.

Characteristics of Japanese leaders: factor items

Factor analysis (varimax rotation) was utilized, identifying the following items in the factor clusters presented below. The alpha coefficient is used as the reliability measure. Factors with alpha scores of 0.65 and above are considered as acceptable.

Policy maker

Discipline　　　　　　　　　　　　　　　*Alpha coefficient 0.74*
- I am very satisfied with my job.
- Most people at my level are satisfied with the job.
- Others think I can be emotional in the way I react and behave. (−)
- I am regularly informed about how new development and initiatives are progressing.
- Many of my colleagues do not understand my part of the business. (−)
- I do not really feel stretched in this job. (−)
- My colleagues see me as a mature and tolerant individual.
- So much is happening in the organization, that I lose track of certain new initiatives. (−)
- I am easy to talk to.
- I feel like leaving this job. (−)
- Others value me for my expertise.

Focus　　　　　　　　　　　　　　　　*Alpha coefficient 0.73*
- A well-run, disciplined organization is fundamental to success.
- Maintaining group cohesion demands the constant encouragement of my colleagues to work as a team.
- It is important to follow established work procedures.
- I like people to be tidy and well disciplined.
- We need a structured and disciplined way of managing the business.
- I like people to pay attention to details.
- I respect people who stick to the rules.

Communication   *Alpha coefficient 0.66*
- People should manage their own problems without having to talk them through with others. (−)
- The systems and controls in this organization are a hindrance to me. (−)
- I like to be left alone to do work as I see fit. (−)
- I can talk more easily with people from a similar background.
- I resent being told what to do. (−)
- Checking out my plans with others slows me down rather than adds anything of value. (−)
- I enjoy getting others to understand some of the more technical aspects of my job.

Driver

Results orientation   *Alpha coefficient 0.77*
- I expect to be kept informed of progress on agreed initiatives.
- Monitoring group cohesion demands the constant encouragement of my colleagues to work as a team.
- No matter what you feel, it is important to show you are calm under pressure.
- A well-run, disciplined organization is fundamental to success.
- The sort of people we need in this organization must be committed to making the business profitable.
- There is a right and wrong way of doing things.
- I like people to be tidy and well disciplined.
- I insist on being regularly briefed concerning new initiatives.
- We need a structured and disciplined way of managing the business.
- I enjoy the challenge of my role in the company.
- I do not like others to interfere in what I do.
- To ensure that policies are successfully implemented depends on my ability to handle the top team.
- Senior management need to be more disciplined at follow through.
- I like to get my own way.

Implementor

Order   *Alpha coefficient 0.72*
- A disciplined organization is fundamental to success.
- Maintaining group cohesion demands the constant encouragement to work as a team.
- Much of my work satisfaction comes from understanding the technical/specialist side of the job.
- The traditions of the company should be respected.

- It is important to follow established work procedures.
- I can talk more easily with people from a similar technical background than with those from other functions.
- I like people to be tidy and well disciplined.
- We need a structured and disciplined way of managing the business.
- I respect people who stick to the rules.

Organization satisfaction   *Alpha coefficient 0.66*
- Others think I can be emotional in the way I behave. (−)
- The systems and controls in this organization are a hindrance to me. (−)
- The company has been misguided in many of the changes it has carried out. (−)
- Most of the changes within the company have been for the best.
- It takes time for people to really get to know me. (−)
- Senior executives in this organization could be more tolerant of each other. (−)
- I do not feel stretched in this job. (−)
- I feel like leaving this job. (−)

Follow through   *Alpha coefficient 0.66*
- Senior management need to be more disciplined at follow through. (−)
- I am committed to this organization.
- I am easy to talk to.
- I encourage subordinates to discuss their work problems with me.
- People talk to me about their work problems.
- I am disciplined at follow through.

Consensus   *Alpha coefficient 0.68*
- People should manage their own problems without having to talk them through with others. (−)
- I like to be left alone to do my work as I see fit. (−)
- I like being in a position where others do not have control over me. (−)
- I resent being told what to do. (−)
- I am more likely to do what I think best and observe the protocol later. (−)
- Being my own boss is what really turns me on. (−)
- Checking out my plans with others slows me down rather than adds anything of value.

References

Abegglen, J. C. (1958) 'The Japanese factory', in M. Takanashi (ed.), (1994) *Kawaru nihongata koyô (Japan's Changing Employment System)*, Tokyo: Nihon Keizai Shinbunsha.

Abegglen, J. C. and Stalk, Jr, G. (1985) *Kaisha: The Japanese Corporation*, New York: Basic Books.

Ackroyd, S., Burrel, G., Hughes, M. and Whitaker, A. (1988) 'The Japanisation of British industry?', *Industrial Relations Journal* spring: 11–23.

Akutagawa, M. (1994) *Yakuin no hôritsu Kokoroe (What Directors Need to Know about the Law)*, Tokyo: Nihon Hôrei.

Aonuma, Y. (1965) *Nihon no keieisô (Japan's Executive Stratum)*, Tokyo: Nihon Keizai Shinbunsha.

Aso, M. and Amano, I. (1978) *Education and Japan's Modernization*, London: Ministry of Foreign Affairs, Embassy of Japan.

Atarashi, M. (1992) *Ichiryû no shidôsha (The First-Class Leaders)*, Tokyo: Kanki Shuppan.

Ballon, R. J. and Tomita, I. (1988) *The Financial Behaviour of Japanese Corporations*, Tokyo and New York: Kôdansha International.

Bank of Japan (1994) *Wagakuni no koyô seido ni tsuite (On Japan's Employment System)*, *Rôsei Jihô* 8 April: 34–8.

Bennis, W. and Nanus, B. (1985) *Leaders: The strategies for Taking Change*, New York: Harper & Row.

Bjorkman, I. and Gernsten, M. (1990) 'Corporate expatriation: an analysis of firms and country specific differences in Scandinavia', unpublished paper.

Bownas, G. and Dickinson, D. (1972) *The Asian Phoenix*, London: BBC.

Bratton, J. (1992) *Japanization at Work*, London: Macmillan.

Brewster, C. (1989) 'Employee relations training for expatriate managers', *Journal of European and Industrial Training* 4(6): 7–11.

Brewster, C., Lundmark, A. and Holden, L. (1991) *A Different Tack*, London: Kogan Page.

Chûma, H. (1994) *Nihongata koyô chôsei (Japanese-type Employment Adjustment)*, Tokyo: Shûeisha.

Clark, R. (1979) *The Japanese Company*, New Haven and London: Yale University Press.

Crump, L. (1989a) 'Japanese managers – Western workers: cross-cultural training and development issues', *Journal of Management Development* 8(4): 48–55.

Crump, L. (1989b) 'Planning and strategy in Japanese–Western negotiations', *The Study of Business and Industry*, College of Commerce, Nihon University, no. 6, 476–92.

Dertouzos, M. L., Lester, R. K. and Solow, R. M. (1989) *Made in America – Regaining the Productive Edge*, Cambridge, Mass.: MIT Press.

Dore, R. P. (1965) *Education in Tokugawa Japan*, London: Routledge & Kegan Paul.

Dore, R. P. (1987) *Taking Japan Seriously*, London: Athlone.

Edstrom, A. and Galbraith, J. (1977) 'Transfer of managers as a co-ordination and control strategy in multi-national corporations', *Administrative Science Quarterly* 22: 248–63.

Emmott, B. (1993) *Japan's Global Reach*, London: Arrow.

Evans, P. (1994) 'The paradox of a world where solutions are looking for problems', *European Forum for Management Development* 3: 67–73.

Everitt, B. B. (1985) *Cluster Analysis*, London: Heinemann.

Fuji Sôgô Kenkyusho (1993) *Main Bank shisutemu oyobi kabushiki ni tsuite no chôsa (An Investigation regarding Main Bank System and Shareholding)*, Tokyo: Research Report.

Gotô, T. (1983) *Nihonteki keiei to bunka (The Japanese-style Management and Culture)*, Tokyo: Gakubunsha.

Guptara, P. (1994) 'Japanese leaders: perception and realities', *Journal of Japanese Trade and Industry* 1: 36–8.

Hall, J. W. (1968) 'The castle town and Japan's modern urbanization', in J. W. Hall and M. B. Jansen (eds) *Studies in the Institutional History of Early Modern Japan*, Princeton: Princeton University Press.

Hanill, J. (1989) 'Expatriate policies in British multi-nationals', *Journal of General Management* 14(4): 18–33.

Harada, K. (1994) *Kakaku kakumei – Nihon kigyôno chôsen (Cost Revolution – The Challenge of the Japanese Company)*, Tokyo: Nihon Keizai Shinbunsha.

Hatakeyama, Y. (1992) *Torishimariyaku to Jigyô Buchô (The Directors and Business Division Leaders – Their Responsibilities and Functions)*, Tokyo: Nihon Nôritsu Kyôkai Manejimento Sentâ.

Hayashida, M. (1995) 'PL taiô, jôhô sentâ de' ('Product liability claims to be dealt with by the information centres'), *Nihon Keizai Shinbun* 30 June: 29.

Hazama, H. (1963) *Nihonteki keiei no keihu (Genealogy of the Japanese-style Management)*, Tokyo: Nihon Nôritsu Kyôkai.

Hedland, G. (1986) 'The hypermodern MNC – a hierarchy?' *Human Resource Management* 25(1): 9–35.

Higashide, K. (1995) 'Kôshu ga rokudai kigyô-shûdan o chûshi suru wake' ('The reasons why the Fair Trading Commission pays close attention to the activities of the six major business groupings'), *Ekonomisuto* 30 May: 51–5.

Honma, M. (1994) *Shin nihongata keiei sisutemu (New Japanese-type Management System)*, Tokyo: TBS Buritanica.

Hori, K. (1994) *Howaito-karâ kaizô keikaku (Planning for the Remaking of White-collar Workers)*, Tokyo: Asahi Shinbunsha.

Hunter, J. E. (1989) *The Emergence of Modern Japan*, London: Longman.

Igarashi, H. (1995) 'Kyû-Zaibatsukei sandai gurûpu no meian – Mitsubishi gurûpu' ('The fortunes of the three pre-war *zaibatsu* business groupings – the case of the Mitsubishi group'), *Ekonomisuto* 30 May: 34–6.

Ikeya, A. (1994) 'Bank profits plunge: write-offs increase', *Nikkei Weekly*, June.

Institute of Productivity Studies (1993) *Kigyo ni okeru toppu ishikettei no arikata ni tsuite (The Process of Decision Making by the Top Management in Industry)*, questionnaire survey, Tokyo: Japan Productivity Centre, 16 July.

Institute of Productivity Studies (1994) *Shûshin koyô-seido no shôrai yosoku chôsa hôkokusho (A Report on the Survey on the Prediction of the Future of the Lifetime Employment System – Outlook and Choice in the Employment System in Japan)*, Nihon Seisansei Honbu (Japan Productivity Centre), January.

Ishida, H. (1986) 'Transferability of Japanese human resource management abroad', *Human Resource Management* 25(1): 103–20.

Itami, H. (1990) *Jinpon-shugi kigyô* (*The Human Capitalist Corporation*), Tokyo: Chikuma Shobô, 7th edition.

Itami, H. (1991) 'Kigyô no toppu senshutsu to chekku' ('Selection of top management and checking system in the company), Economics Series, *Yomiuri Shinbun* 26 August.

Itami, H. (1993) *Manejimento fairu '93 – Kigyô wa dareno monoka* (*Management File, 1993 – Who Owns the Company?*), Tokyo: NTT Shuppan.

Itami, H. *et al.* (1993) *Nihon no ginkôgyô – hontôni hatten shitanoka* (*The Banking Industry in Japan – Did It Really Prosper*), Tokyo: NTT Shuppan.

Ito, K. (1993a) 'Kabushiki Mochiai – sono rasengata rojikku' ('Cross-shareholding: a spiral logic'), in H. Itami, T. Kagono and M. Ito (eds) *Nihon no kigyô shisutemu: Dai-ikkan – Kigyô to wa Nanika* (*Japanese Enterprise System: Series 1 – What is an Enterprise?*), Tokyo: Yûhikaku.

Ito, K. (1993b) 'Nihon no kaisha seido to chekku kikô – Aratana Nihongata moderu o motomete' ('The corporate structure and checking system in Japan: in search of a new Japanese model'), *Hitotsubashi Business Review* 40(3): 1–17.

Iwata, R. (1977) *Nihonteki keiei no hensei genri* (*The Structural Principle of Japanese-style Management*), Tokyo: Bunshindô.

Jackson, T. (1993) *Turning Japanese – The Fight for Industrial Control of the New Europe*, London: HarperCollins.

Japan Management Association (1994a) 'Nihonteki jinji sisutemu no ridezain' ('Redesigning the Japanese-style personnel system – an angle on innovative changes on organisation and personnel towards supra-Japanese-type management'), *Nihon Noritsu Kyokai* March.

Japan Management Association (1994b) *Kigyô o sasaeru bijinesu riidâ ikusei no tameno jinji sisutemu no arikata ni kansuru chôsa* (*A Summary Report on the Survey on the Personnel System Designed for Development of Business Leaders*), Japan Management Association, 16th Annual Survey of Management Issues, November.

Japan Productivity Centre (Nihon Seisausei Honbu) (1989) *Seisansei Modern Sogo chingin chosa hokokusho* (*Report on a Survey of Comprehensive Compensations by Productivity Models*) Tokyo: Japan Productivity Centre.

Jaques, E. (1951) *The Changing Culture of the Factory*, London: Tavistock.

JETRO (ed.) (1994) 'Nippon – business facts and figures', *JETRO* (annual statistical booklet).

JETRO (1995) 'JETRO White Paper on foreign direct investment', *JETRO*, March.

Johnson, C. (1988) 'Japanese-style management in America', *California Management Review* 30(4): 34–45.

Kagaku Gijutsu Chô (ed.) (1982) *Kagaku Gijutsu Hakusho – Kokusai hikaku no kongo to kadai* (*1998 Annual Science and Technology White Paper on International Comparison and Future Themes*) Tokyo: Ôkurashô.

Kagono, T. (1994) 'Kigyô ni okeru tekisetsuna gabanansu towa' ('What is the appropriate governance in the corporation?') *Proceedings of the 1994 Annual Conference*, Soshiki Gakkai, 45–50.

Kagono, T. (1995) 'PL-hô o maemuki ni' ('Respond to product liability law positively'), *Nihon Keizai Shinbun*, 30 June.

Kakabadse, A. P. (1991a) 'Effectiveness at the top: preliminary analysis of 32 European organisations', in C. Brewster and S. Tyson (eds) *International Comparisons in Human Relations Management*, London: Pitman, 227–39.

Kakabadse, A. P. (1994) 'Japan: about turn not down turn', *Management Focus*, Cranfield University, School of Management, summer.

Kakabadse, A. P. and Myers, A. (1996) 'Boardroom skills for Europe', *European Management Journal* forthcoming.

Kakabadse, A. P., Okazaki-Ward, L. I. and Myers, A. (1995) 'Leadership in times of change: towards stakeholder value – a Cranfield comparative study of top Japanese/European managers', in S. Tyson (ed.) *Strategic Prospects for HRM*, London: Institute of Personnel and Development, Chapter 6.

Keieijuku (1994) 'Tsuini Daiei no gunmon ni kudatta ôte kaden meekâ' ('Major home electric manufacturers make concessions to Daiei'), *Keieijuku* June: 21.

Keieijuku (1995a) 'Masseki jômu, Idei Shinnosuke ga sekai no Sonî no shachô o itomeru made' ('How Idei, the most junior of the executive directors, hit the president's post'), *Keieijuku* May: 34–9.

Keieijuku (1995b) 'Yakuin kanbu o tairyô irekaeshita, kôkokugyôkai no garibâ – Dentsû' ('Dentsû – Gulliver of the advertising industry which saw a large turnover of the directors in its board'), *Keieijuku* August: 38–41.

Keizai Dôyûkai (1994a) *Dai 11-kai Kigyô Hakusho – Henkakuki no Kigyô Keiesha (The 11th White Paper on the Enterprise – The Top Management Team in the Time of Change)*, Tokyo: Keizai Doyukai, January.

Keizai Dôyûkai (1994b) *Japanese Management for the 21st Century – Establishment of Corporate Selfhood and Creative Management*, Tokyo: Keizai Doyukai, January.

Keizai Dôyûkai (1994c) 'Teigen-Kojin to Kigyô no jirirsu to chôwa' ('A proposal: self-regulation and harmony between the individuals and the company'), *Keizai Doyuai* May.

Keizai Kôhô Centre (1982–95) *Japan: An International Comparison*, Tokyo: Keizai Kôhô Centre.

Kobayashi, H. (1994) 'Too many unnecessary human resources: towards an early revision of seniority and other practices', *Yomiuri Newspaper* 10 October: 11.

Kon'ya, N. (1995) 'Kabushiki mochiai wa hikôritsu demo fukôhei demo nai' ('Cross-shareholding is neither inefficient nor unfair'), *Ekonomisuto* 30 May: 62–4.

Kôshiro, K. (1994) 'Nenkô chingin no kenshô to korekarano hôkôsei' ('An examination of the seniority-based wages and its future direction'), *Rôsei Jihô* 3,158 (15 April): 72–7.

Kotter, J. P. (1982) *The General Managers*, New York: Free Press.

Kouzes, J. and Posner, B. (1993) *Credibility: How Leaders Gain and Lose It, Why People Demand It*, New York: Macmillan.

Koyô Kaihatsu Sentâ (1994) 'Howaitokarâ kara mita jinji rômu eno kitai' ('Expectations for personnel measures by the white-collar workers'), *Rôsei Jihô* 3,158 (15 April).

Kudo, H., Tachikawa, T. and Suzuki, N. (1988) 'How US and Japanese CEOs spend their time', *Long Range Planning* 21/6(112): 79–82.

Lincoln, E. J. (1993) *Japan's New Global Role*, Washington DC: The Brookings Institution.

Magota Rôhei (1994) 'Nenkô shogû, chingin no saiseisaku' ('Measures for the revival of seniority-based conditions of work and pay'), *Rôsei Jihô* 3,158 (15 April): 67–71.

Mannari, H. (1974) *The Japanese Business Leaders*, Tokyo: University of Tokyo Press.

Margerison, C. J. (1980) 'How chief executives succeed', *Journal of European and Industrial Training* 3(3) (monograph).

Margerison, C. J. and Lewis, R. (1983) 'Mapping managerial work preferences', *The Journal of Management Development* 2(1): 36–50.

Margerison, C. J. and Kakabadse, A. P. (1984) 'How American chief executives succeed: implications for developing high potential employees', *American Management Association Survey Report*.

Masui, K. (1994) 'The lessons from the mistakes made in international business', *Manejimento 21*, Japan Management Association, June, 12–27.

Mauser, F. F. and Stewart, D. J. (1982) *American Business: An Introduction*, New York: Harcourt Brace Jovanovich.

Minami, R. (1994) *The Economic Development of Japan: A Quantitative Study*, London: Macmillan.

Ministry of Finance Study Group (1993) 'The Bubble: why it happened, why it burst, what it wrought', *Nikkei Weekly* 12 April.

Mintzberg, H. (1973) *The Nature of Managerial Work*, New York: Harper & Row.

Mishima, Y. (1979) *Mitsubishi zaibatsu-shi (History of the Mitsubishi Zaibatsu)*, Tokyo: Kyôikusha.

Mochizuki, K. (1994) 'Tomorrow's capitalism in a Japanese perspective', *Royal Society of Arts Journal* 142(5,453): 37–46.

Morikawa, H. (1978) *Nihon zaibatsu-shi (History of Japanese Zaibatsu)* Tokyo: Kyôikusha.

Morikawa, H. (1981) *Nihon Keiei-shi (History of Japanese Management)*, Tokyo: Nihon Keizai Shinbunsa.

Nakamura, T. (1981) *The Postwar Japanese Economy – Its Development and Structure*, Tokyo: University of Tokyo Press.

Nihon Keiei Kyokai (1990) 'Nichi-bei-oo toppu manejimento no ishiki hikaku chôsa' ('Report on a comparative study of management attitudes in Japan, the US and Europe'), *Nihon Keiei Kyokai* (NOMA Institute) January.

Nihon Keieisha Dantai Renmei (1995) *Shinjidai no 'Nihonteki keiei' – Chôsen subeki hôkô to sono gutaisaku ('Japanese-style Management' in a New Era – The Direction and the Practical Measures)*, Tokyo: Nihon Keieisha Dantai Renmei (Nikkeiren) May.

Nihon Keizai Shinbun (1994) 'Kunô suru Shin-nittetsu' ('Nippon steel in distress'), *Nihon Keizai Shinbun* 16 June: 13.

Nihon Keizai Shinbunsha (ed.) (1992) *Kabushiki torihiki no chishiki (How to Play the Stock Market)*, Tokyo: Nihon Keizai Shinbunsha.

Nihon Keizai Shinbunsha (ed.) (1993) *Ginkô hutô shinwa no hôkai (The Crumbling of the Myth of Banks Never Bankrupting)*, Tokyo: Nihon Keizai Shinbunsha.

Nihon Keizai Shinbunsha (ed.) (1994) *Nihongata jinji wa owatta – Yakushoku defure jidai no tôrai (The End of the Japanese-type Personnel Practices – Arrival of the 'Period of Management-post Deflation')*, Tokyo: Nihon Keizai Shinbunsha.

Nihon Keizai Shinbun (1995) 'Kabuyasu-endaka – Akujunkan no Nihon keizai: Jô – sokotsuku kabushiki fukumieti' ('Low share prices/high yen – Japanese economy suffering from the vicious circle: Part 1 – the hidden profit from the shares scraping the bottom of the barrel'), *Nihon Keizai Shinbun* 24 March: 1.

Nihon Keizai Shinbun (1995) 'Kabushiki mochiai – kawaru kôzô: Kaishô no ugoki kasoku' ('Cross-shareholding – changing structure: 1 – quickening pace of cancellation'), *Nihon Keizai Shinbun* 6 April: 15.

Nihon Keizai Shinbun (1995) 'Kabushiki mochiai – kawaru kôzô: Keiei, ROE jûshi e' ('Cross-shareholding – changing structure: 2 – shift of management emphasis to ROE'), *Nihon Keizai Shinbun* 7 April: 15.

Nihon Keizai Shinbun (1995) 'Endaka no baransu shiito: 1' ('Balance sheet on the high yen: Pt 1'), *Nihon Keizai Shinbun* 18 April: 5.

Nihon Keizai Shinbun (1995) 'Mini kabushiki shijô – Toyota 16-man yen, Shin-Nittetsu wa 3-man yen de') ('The mini-stock market – Y160,000 for the minimum Toyota shares, and Y30,000 for the minimum Japan Steel Corporation's shares'), *Nihon Keizai Shinbun* 19 April: 3.

Nihon Keizai Shinbun (1995) 'Chô-endaka – Keieisha ni kiku – Jidôsha: Toyota' ('Super high yen – opinion of the top management – Automobile/Toyota'), *Nihon Keizai Shinbun* 19 April: 13.

Nihon Keizai Shinbun (1995) 'Shijô kasseika ni "mini kabushiki shijô" katsuyô o' ('Utilizing the mini-stock market for enlivening the capital market'), *Nihon Keizai Shinbun* 20 April: 2.

Nihon Keizai Shinbun (1995) 'Ekidashi de anaume – eikyô husegu – huryôsaiken shôkyaku ni okuremo' ('Make up the loss by the sale of shares thereby keeping a healthy balance sheet – delay in the clearing of bad debts feared'), *Nihon Keizai Shinbun* 25 April: 7.

Nihon Keizai Shinbun (1995) 'Nippon no keiei – hukumi ga kieta – 1: mochiai no yumekara samete' ('Management in Japan – the disappearing unrealized profit – 1: awakening from the dream world of cross-shareholding'), *Nihon Keizai Shinbun* 25 April: 13.

Nihon Keizai Shinbun (1995) 'Nihon no keiei – hukumi ga kieta' ('Japanese management – disappearing hidden profit'), *Nihon Keizai Shinbun* 25 April: 1.

Nihon Keizai Shinbun (1995) 'Togin huryôsaiken – mishorigaku 8chô 8sen-oku-en' ('Bad debts by the city banks – Y8.8 trillion in unsettled amounts'), *Nihon Keizai Shinbun* 30 April: 1.

Nihon Keizai Shinbun (1995) 'Chô-endaka – Toyota no Sentaku: Jô ('Super-high yen – the choice for Toyota: Pt 1'), *Nihon Keizai Shinbun* 4 May: 1.

Nihon Keizai Shinbun (1995) 'Chô-endaka – Toyota no sentaku: Chû' ('Super-high yen – the choice for Toyota: Pt 2'), *Nihon Keizai Shinbun* 5 May: 1.

Nihon Keizai Shinbun (1995) 'Jidôsha Nichibei jisshitsu gôi' ('US–Japan substantive agreement on motor vehicles'), *Nihon Keizai Shinbun* 29 June: 1.

Nihon Keizai Shinbun (1995) 'Saita no 2,110sha, issei ni kabunushisôkai' ('Shareholders' Annual General Meeting – 2,110 firms, the largest number ever, hold it on the same day'), *Nihon Keizai Shinbun* 30 June: 7.

Nihon Keizai Shinbun (1995) 'Keiei no shiten – nichibei kôshô kara kigyô ga manabukoto' ('Perspective on management – a lesson to be learned by corporations from the US–Japan negotiations'), *Nihon Keizai Shinbun* 2 July: 7.

Nihon Keizai Shinbun (1995) 'Gaikokujin mochikabu hiritsu – 2nen renzoku kako saikôni' ('Percentage of shares held by foreigners – the highest ever in second year in succession'), *Nihon Keizai Shinbun* 15 July: 1.

Nihon Keizai Shinbun (1996), 'Hashimoto ninki ni reisui' ('Pour cold water on the Hashimoto popularity'), *Jusen*, 12 March: 3. Related article also on p. 1.

Nihon Rôdô Kenkyû Kikô (1994) 'Howaitokarâ no idô to shôshin ni kansuru chôsa' ('A survey on the rotation and promotion of the white-collar workers'), *Rôsei Jihô* 3,158 (15 April): 5–12.

Nihon Sangyô Kunren Kyôkai (1971) *Sangyô Kanren Hyakunen-shi* (*One Hundred Year History of Industrial Training*), Tokyo: Nihon Sangyô Kunren Kyôkai (JIVTA).

Nihon Seisansei Honbu (1994) 'Shûshin koyô seido no shôrai yosoku chôsa – waga kuni koyôseido no tenbô to yosoku' ('A survey on the future prospects of the "lifetime" employment system – the outlook and prediction of employment system in Japan'), *Rôsei Jihô* 8 April: 18–25.

Nihon Seisansei Honbu Keiei Akademii (1994) 'Posuto Nenkô chingin – nendaibetsu, kôsubetsu chingin seido o teisho' ('Post-Nenkô wages – advocacy for a wages system based on age and streams'), *Rôsei Jihô* 3,158 (15 April): 65–6.

Nikkei Business (1994) 'Soshô no kyôfu – riigaru maindo ga kaisha o sukuu' ('The terror of being taken to court – knowledge of law that saves the corporations'), *Nikkei Business* 9 May: 11–27.

Nikkei Weekly (1995) 'The yen's surge raises prospect of Japan as world's largest economy', *Nikkei Weekly* 24 April.

Nikkeiren (1994) 'Shin Nihonteki keiei sisutemu tô kenkyû purojekuto – chûkan hôkoku' ('A research project on new Japanese-style management system and related matters – the interim report'), *Nikkeiren Taimusu* 18 August.

Nomura Research Institute (1994) 'Shin-nihonteki koyô shisutemu ni tsuite' ('On a new Japanese-style employment system'), *Rôsei Jihô* 8 April: 39–41.

Nomura Sôgô Kenkyûsho (1992) 'Nihon kigyô no kôporêto Gabanansu' ('Corporate governance of Japanese companies'), *Zaikai Kansoku* September.

Ogishima, S. (1993) 'Kabushiki mochiai ga kabuka keisei ni ataeru eikyô' ('The influence of cross-shareholding on share prices'), Nihon Shôken Analyst Kyôkai, *Shôken Anaristo* June.

Ohta, Y. (1994) *Kin'yû taikoku nihon no chôraku* (*The Fall of Japan, the Financial Giant*), Tokyo: Nihon Keizai Shinbunsha.

Okazaki-Ward, L. I. (1993) *Management Education and Training in Japan*, London: Graham & Trotman.

Okochi, K., Karsh, B. and Levine, S. B. (1973) *Workers and Employers in Japan*, Tokyo: University of Tokyo Press.

Okuda, K. (1994) 'Antei Koyô no konseputo o teishô – Shûshin koyô wa gokai maneku' ('Suggestion of an alternative concept: stable employment – "lifetime employment" breeds misunderstanding'), *Rôsei Jihô* 8 April: 7–12.

Okumura, H. (1991) *Shinpan hôjin shihonshugi no kôzô* (*The Structure of Corporate Capitalism – A New Edition*), Tokyo: Shakai Shisôsha.

Okumura, H. (1994a) 'Kaitai shihajimeteiru shûshin koyo' ('The "lifetime employment" which is beginning to disintegrate'), *Rôsei Jihô* 8 April: 13–17.

Okumura, H. (1994b) *Kaitai suru 'keiretsu' to hôjin shihonshugi* (*Dissolving 'Keiretsu' and Corporatist Capitalism*), Tokyo: Shakai Shisôsha.

Okamura, H. (1995) *Hôjin shihonshugi no unmei – Kabushiki kaisha no 'shini itaru yamai'* (*The Future of the Corporatist Capitalism – 'The Fatal Disease' of Japanese Corporations*), Tokyo: Tôyô Keizai Shinpôsha.

Okumura, H. and Sataka, M. (1992) *Kigyô jiken-shi – Nihonteki Keiei no omote to ura* (*History of Corporate Affairs – The Frontage and Behind the Scenes of the Japanese-style Management*), Tokyo: Shakai Shisôsha.

Okumura, H. *et al.* (1994) *Kigyô tanken – nihon kabushiki kaisho no 'seiiki' ni idomu* (*Exploration of the Japanese Corporation – Penetration into the 'Sacred Zone' of the Japanese Limited Companies*), Tokyo: Shakai Shisôsha.

Oliver, N. and Wilkinson, B. (1990) *The Japanisation of British Industry*, Oxford: Blackwell.

Omura Keiichi (1993) *Kabushiki Mochiai no ishiki kôzô* (*How do Japanese Companies Consider Cross-Shareholding?*), Report of International Finance Group, Tokyo: Keiei Academy.

Oshima, M. and Kubota, M. (1994) *Kiken na keieisha – shippai ni manabanai mono wa horobiru* (*The Dangerous Top Management – Those Who Do Not Learn from Mistakes Will be Destroyed*), Tokyo: Nihon Keizai Shinbunsha.

Rômu Gyôsei Kenkyûsho (1994a) 'Jinji kachô ankeeto – shûshin koyô-sei ni taisuru kaitô riyû' ('A questionnaire survey of personnel section chiefs – a list of reasons as to why they answered in that way to questions on the "lifetime employment" system'), *Rôsei Jihô* 8 April: 42–4.

Rômu Gyôsei Kenkyûsho (1994b) 'Jinji kachô ankeeto – nenkô chingin seido no yukue ni taisuru kaitô naiyô ichiranhyo' ('A questionnaire survey of personnel section chiefs – a list of answers to questions on the future direction of the seniority-based wages system'), *Rôsei Jihô* 3,158 (15 April): 63–4.

Rôsei Jihô (1994a) 'Howaitokarâ jinji kanri no genjô to kongo no hôkô' ('Personnel management of white-collar workers now and its future direction'), *Rôsei Jihô* 3,158 (15 April): 2–56.

Rôsei Jihô (1994b) 'Nihonteki keiei no kenshô to sono mirai – 1: Shûshin koyô no hôkai wa susumu ka – chûmoku sareru sono yukue' ('Examination of the Japanese-style management and its future – 1: will the break-up of "lifetime" employment proceed? – its direction to be watched'), *Rôsei Jihô* 3,157 (8 April): 2–44.

Rôsei Jihô (1994c) 'Nihonteki keiei no kenshô to sono mirai – 2: nenkô chingin-sei no hôkai wa susumu ka – chûmoku sareru sono yukue' ('Examination of the Japanese-style management and its future – 2: will the breakdown of seniority-based wages system proceed? Its direction to watch'), *Rôsei Jihô* 3,158 (15 April): 57–77.

Rostow, W. W. (1960) *The Stages of Economic Growth: A Non-Communist Manifesto*, London: Cambridge University Press.

Rummel, R. J. (1970) *Applied Factor Analysis*, Evanston: Northwestern University Press.

Sakudô, Y. (1979) *Sumitomo zaibatsu-shi (History of the Sumitomo 'Zaibatsu')*, Tokyo: Kyôikusha.

Sangyôkunren Hakusho Henshû Iinkai (ed.) (1971) *Sangyô kunren hyakunen-shi (A Hundred Year History of Industrial Training)*, Tokyo: Nihon Sangyô Kunren Kyôkai.

Sano, Y. (1993) 'Changes and continued stability in Japanese HRM systems: choice in the share economy', *The International Journal of Human Resource Management* 4(1): 11–27.

Sataka, M. (1992) *Kaisha wa dareno mono ka – kigyô no seshû to dokusai hihan (To Whom Does the Corporation Belong? – Critique of Private Succession and Dictatorship)*, Tokyo: Shakai Shisôsha.

Sataka, M. (1993) *Kigyô Genron (The Principle of the Business Organization)*, Tokyo: Shakai Shisôsha.

Sataka, M. (1994) *Tôsei kigyô annai (Introduction to Today's Corporations)*, Tokyo: Shakai Shisôsha.

Schuler, R. S. and Dowling, P. J. (1988) *Survey of ASPA/I Members*, New York: Stern School of Business, New York University.

Seimei Hoken Bunka Sentaa (1994) 'Shûshin koyô ni kansuru hyôka to ikô – [shûrô ishiki ni kansuru chôsa]' ('Evaluation and views on "lifetime" employment – "A Survey concerning Approach to Work"', *Rôsei Jihô* 8 April: 31–3.

Sekine, J. (1994) *Toppu-daun no keiei (Top-down Management)*, Tokyo: Nihon Keizai Shinbunsha.

Shibagaki, K. (1965) *Nihon kin'yûshihon bunseki (Analysis of Financial Capital in Japan)*, Tokyo: University of Tokyo Press.

Shigeta, I. and Morita, Y. (1994) 'Areru risutora no arashi – yakuin wa mukizu ka' ('Blowing gale of restructuring – are the executives unaffected?'), *Yomiuri Shinbun* 10 October: 11.

Shima, K. (1991) *Kin'yu seido no hanashi (Financial Systems in Japan)*, Tokyo: Nihon Keizai Shinbunsha.

Shimada, H. (1994) *Nihon no koyô – 21-seiki eno saisekkei (Japanese Employment – Re-designing towards the 21st century)*, Tokyo: Chikuma Shobô.

Shimizu, R. (1986) *Top Management in Japanese Firms*, Tokyo: Chikura Shobô.

Shimizu, R. (1989) *The Japanese Business Success Factors*, Tokyo: Chikura Shobô.

Shimizu, R. (1992) *Company Vitalization by Top Management in Japan*, Tokyo: Keiô Tsûshin.

Shimizu, M., Kakabadse, A. P. and Okazaki-Ward, L. I. (1994) 'Kigyô toppu chiimu no Keieikôdô ni kansuru Keieisha/yakuin chôsa – gai yô hôkoku' ('A survey of corporate leaders and their management behaviour'), *Summary Report of the Institute of Innovative Management*, Japan Management Association, October.

Stewart, R. C. (1982) *Choices for the Manager: A Guide to Managerial Work*, London: McGraw-Hill.

Sugiyama, C. and Mizuta, H. (1988) *Enlightenment and Beyond – Political Economy Comes to Japan*, Tokyo: University of Tokyo Press.

Suzuki, N. (1986) 'Strategic profile of engineering and non-engineering CEO-led companies: the US and Japan', in R. N. Farmer (ed.), *Advance in International Comparative Management*, Connecticut: JAI Press, 69–83.

Suzuki, N. (1989) 'Attributes of Japanese CEOs: can they be trained?', *Journal of Management Development* 8(4): 5–11.

Suzuki, T. (1994) 'Yameruyori sekinin hatase – herashisugi wa shiki ni hibiku' ('Meet the responsibility rather than resign – too drastic a reduction in the number of directors will affect morale'), *Yomiuri Shinbun* 10 October: 11.

Takami, S. (1994) 'Kunôsusu Shinnittetsu – Jin'in seiri mattanashi' ('Japan Steel Corporation in turmoil – no time to waste for personnel cost reduction'), *Nihon Keizai Shinbun* 16 June.

Takanashi, M. (1994) *Kawaru Nihon gata koyô (Japan's Changing Employment System)*, Tokyo: Nihon Keizai Shinbunsha.

Takeda, K. (1992) *Riidâshippu o mini tsukeru – Hito o sodateru kôdôgaku (How to Cultivate Leadership – Learning Through Behavioural Sciences)*, Tokyo: Nihon Seisansei Honbu.

Tanaka, F. (1993a) 'The impact of introducing international accounting standards', *Tokyo Business Today* May: 18–21.

Tanaka, F. (1993b) 'Whose company is it anyway controversy', *Tokyo Business Today* August: 14–16.

Terasawa Mizuho (1995) 'Split nationality – humiliating treaties left Japanese psyche divided', *Japan Update* March: 20–1.

Tokyo Business Today (1993) 'From "lifetime employment" to the expendable salaryman?' *Tokyo Business Today* May: 8–10.

Tokyo Business Today (1993) 'On the corporate dole: Japan's one million "Working Unemployed"', *Tokyo Business Today* May: 10–11.

Tokyo Business Today Panel Discussion (1994) '"Time-server" directors – do your company a favour: quit', *Tokyo Business Today* November: 32–4.

Tokyo Chamber of Commerce and Industry (1994) 'Koyô kanri no jittai to jinji seisaku ni kansuru chôsa' ('A survey concerning the state of employment management and personnel policy'), *Rôsei Jihô* 8 April: 26–30.

Tokyo Kanrishoku Union (1994) *Kaisha o yameru chichi kara kaisha ni hairu musoko, musumetachi e (To Our Sons and Daughters about to Enter Kaisha from Fathers who Are Leaving It)*, Tokyo: Kyôiku Shiryô Shuppankai.

Torao, S., Kawashima, S., Isoyama, T. and Kubori, H. (1994) 'Soshô hokyôhu – rigaru maindo ga kigyo o sukuu' ('The terror of legal action – legal preparedness that saves the company'), *Nikkei Business* 9 May.

Tôyô Shimpôsha (1994) In I. Shigeta and Y. Morita 'Hukiareru riustra – yakuin wa kengai? ('Blowing restructuring storm – can the directors be safe from it? ') *Yomiuri Shinbun* 10 October.

Toyota, T. (1964) *Gaisetsu nihon rekishi (Outline History of Japan)*, Tokyo: Osaka Kyôiku Tosho KK.

Tsuda, M. (1988) *Nihonteki keiei no jinji senryaku (Personnel Strategy in the Japanese-style Management)*, Tokyo: Dôbunkan.

Tung, R. L. (1988) 'Career issues in international assignments', *The Academy of Management Review* 11(3): 241–8.

Tyson, S. (1995) *Strategic Prospects for H.R.M.*, London: IPD.

Uchida, K. (1995) 'Political outlook for the 21st century', *Journal of Japanese Trade and Industry* 4: 13–16.

Uchihashi, K. and Sataka, M. (1994) '*Nihon Kabushiki kaisha' hihan (Critique on the Japanese Corporation)*, Tokyo: Shakai Shisôsha.

Van Wolferen, K. (1989) *The Enigma of Japanese Power*, London: Macmillan.

Vogel, E. (1979) *Japan as Number One*, Cambridge, Mass.: Harvard University Press.

Watanabe, S. and Yamamoto, I. (1992) 'Nihon kigyo no kôporêto gabanansu' ('Corporate governance in the Japanese corporation'), *Zaikai Kansoku*, Nomura Research Institute, September: 2–25.

Whitehill, A. M. (1991) *Japanese Management*, London: Routledge.

Wicken, P. (1987) *The Road to Nissan*, London: Macmillan.

Wiersema, M. F. and Bantel, K. A. (1992) 'Top management team demography and corporate strategic change', *Academy of Management Journal* 35(2): 91–118.

Wiersema, M. F. and Bird, A. (1993) 'Organisational demography in Japanese firms: group heterogeneity, individual dissimilarity and top management team turnover', *Academy of Management Journal* 36(9): 996–1,025.

Womack, J. P., Jones, D. T. and Roos, D. (1990) *The Machine that Changed the World*, New York: Rowson Associates.

Yasuoka, S. (1990) *Zaibatsu no Keieishi – Jinbutsuzô to senryaku (History of the Zaibatsu Management – On Personnel and Strategy)*, Tokyo: Shakai Shisôsha.

Zimmerman, M. A. (1985) *Dealing with the Japanese*, London: George Allen & Unwin.

Subject index

Page numbers appearing in **bold** refer to figures; those in *italic* refer to tables. Subheadings marked with an asterisk (*) relate to international comparisons.

accounting, adoption of international standards 53
age 62, 63–4; post-war changes 13–14; sector differences 87–8, *88*; *see also* demographics
AGM specialists (*Sôkaiya*) 55
AGMs 50, 52, 55
alternative attendance 6
antei kabunushi kôsaku (stable shareholder creation manoeuvring) 21, 22, 54
Anti-Monopoly Law 16
approachability 68, *69*
Asano, emergence as *zaibatsu* 10
asset price expansion 30–4
Association of Corporate Executives (*Keizai Dôyûkai*) 14
associations, employers' 11, 14
attitudes to the company: manufacturing* 99, *100*; retail* 111, *113*, 114; sector differences 89, *89*; services* 122, *125*, 126
auditors 51, 52
Austria, *see* management, international comparisons
automobile industry, *see* motor industry
Ayukawa, emergence as *zaibatsu* 10

Bank of Japan 15
banks: 1950s policies 15; bad debts 35, 38; Bank of Japan's control over 15; group banks' acquisition of shares 21, 33–4; groupings with minor *zaibatsu* 16; 'main bank' system 16,

20; in major groupings (*kigyô shûdan*) *45*; omitted from post-war deconcentration 13; over-loan phenomenon 15–16; performance deterioration 35; shares held by *23*
boards of directors: executive board (*jômukai*) 63; members 51–2; network of directorships 10; power of president 51, 55; restructuring 139; role titles 51; structure 50–1, 63; *see also* Presidents' Clubs
'bubble' 30–4
Buddhism 6
business development: pre-1945 6–11; 1945 to 1958 12–18; 1958 to 1973 18–24; 1973 to 1980 24–8; 1980s 28–34; 1990s 34–54
business drivers 74–5; demographics 72; impact of *82*, *83*; profile 72; results orientation 142, 151
business groupings: changes in structure 20–4; *see also kigyô shûdan*; *zaibatsu*
business sectors, *see* manufacturing sector; retail sector; services sector

CALPERS (California Public Employee Retirement Scheme) 53
cameras, in major groupings (*kigyô shûdan*) *48*
capital accumulation 15
car manufacturing, *see* motor industry
career planning 143–4
cement, in major groupings (*kigyô shûdan*) *48*

Author index